Steve Williams
P9-CPX-729

ADAM HAMILTON

LOVE TO STAY

SEX, GRACE, AND COMMITMENT

Abingdon Press

Nashville

Love to Stay:
Sex, Grace, and Commitment

by Adam Hamilton

Copyright © 2013 by Abingdon Press
All rights reserved.

No part of this work may be reproduced or transmitted in any form or by any means, electronic or mechanical, including photocopying and recording, or by any information storage or retrieval system, except as may be expressly permitted by the 1976 Copyright Act or in writing from the publisher. Requests for permission should be addressed in writing to Abingdon Press, 201 Eighth Avenue South, P.O. Box 801, Nashville, TN 37202-0801 or e-mailed to permissions@abingdonpress.com.

This book is printed on acid-free, elemental chlorine-free paper.
ISBN 978-1-4267-5951-2

Scripture quotations, unless otherwise indicated, are from the New Revised Standard Version of the Bible, copyrighted © 1989 by the Division of Christian Education of the National Council of the Churches of Christ in the United States of America, and are used by permission.

Scripture quotations noted CEB are from the Common English Bible. Copyright © 2011 by the Common English Bible. All rights reserved. Used by permission. www.CommonEnglishBible.com.

Scripture quotations marked "NKJV™" are taken from the New King James Version®. Copyright © 1982 by Thomas Nelson, Inc. Used by permission. All rights reserved.

Scripture quotations marked (NIV) are taken from the Holy Bible, New International Version®, NIV®. Copyright © 1973, 1978, 1984, 2011 by Biblica, Inc.ᴹ Used by permission of Zondervan. All rights reserved worldwide. www.zondervan.com. The "NIV" and "New International Version" are trademarks registered in the United States Patent and Trademark Office by Biblica, Inc.™

Library of Congress Cataloging-in-Publication applied for.

13 14 15 16 17 18 19 20 21 22 — 10 9 8 7 6 5 4 3 2 1

MANUFACTURED IN THE UNITED STATES OF AMERICA

To LaVon,
I love you more now than the day we married.

CONTENTS

INTRODUCTION

There lies within the heart of most human beings a deep longing for close companionship with another — one who is like us, yet mysteriously and sometimes maddeningly different from us. That heartfelt urge has been there from the beginning, and most of us feel it long before we're aware of our sexuality.

When I was in first grade, before I knew anything about adult love or true intimacy, I asked a neighbor girl to marry me. Though we were only imitating the relationships we saw in our parents, there was something wonderful and exciting about that childhood friendship.

I was in sixth grade the first time I kissed a girl. We had been meeting at the Coachlight Skating Rink for several weeks when she began hinting that maybe we should kiss. So, one night while we were waiting for our parents to pick us up, we sneaked behind the rink. I had no idea what I was doing, and she didn't either. When the magic moment came, we banged our teeth together hard enough that it hurt. To top it off, she had bad breath.

This is really gross! I thought. Yet I still liked her and wanted to go steady with her. Eventually we improved our technique, and I came to appreciate the excitement of a kiss.

Then at church, when I was fourteen, I met an amazingly beautiful tomboy named LaVon. We became good friends, but it took me two years to work up my courage and have a friend ask her out for me! We began dating, and I found that she made my heart beat faster. I couldn't wait to spend more time with her. The first time I kissed her, I knew that someday she would be my wife. We married right out of high school.

I brought certain preconceived ideas into our marriage. I imagined it would be an eternal state of bliss, full of loving feelings and constant excitement. We would make love every night, and she would cook breakfast for me every morning. (Yes, it was sexist, but I was seventeen and didn't know any better!) Every day, we would be happier than the day before. We would never fight, and for the rest of our lives we would never, ever stop wanting to be together.

Those illusions lasted forty-eight hours. On the third night of our marriage, I learned that making love every night was not in the cards. The next morning, when we woke up in our small apartment, I asked, "What's for breakfast?" She said, "I don't know about you, but I'm having a Pop Tart."

I'm exaggerating, but not by much. Both of us learned a lot that first year of marriage. Over the thirty years since, we've experienced times when we didn't think it was possible to love each other more, and other times when we could hardly stand each other. There were several periods when we wondered, Is this marriage going to make it? Thankfully, we've had far more times when we were happy to be together. Today our love is stronger than it's ever been, but I know there will be challenges yet to come. That's the reality of marriage—it has its ups and downs, its ebb and flow, and it requires perseverance, hard work, and from time to time a bit of help.

In this book we'll explore the meaning and mission of marriage. I hope to offer an honest, real, and hope-filled picture of the blessings and challenges of marriage, and what it takes to make it work. Though the book focuses on marriage, so many of the principles can also be applied to other committed relationships and to nearly every other relationship in our lives. I offer the book as part encouragement and part coaching, to help you achieve a love that lasts a lifetime.

In sharing my thoughts on the subject, I'll be drawing on several sources: the wisdom of the Scriptures; the knowledge of experts in the field of relationships; a survey of 5,184 people affiliated with the church I pastor; the stories of hundreds of couples who have talked with me over the years about their marriages; and the experience of LaVon and me during thirty years of seeking to love one another.

No coaching is complete without practice. At the end of each chapter, you'll find a short section called "Reflect and Engage," lifting up an important theme presented in the chapter through story, activity, and prayer. You'll find activities for couples to do together and separately, as well as activities for readers who are single.

My hope is that within the Scriptures, stories, statistics, and activities, you will find practical wisdom to help as you and your spouse or loved one learn the lifelong dance that marriage is meant to be.

1

More Than a Piece of Paper

Then the Lord God said, "It is not good that the man should be alone;
I will make him a helper as his partner."…So the Lord God caused a
deep sleep to fall upon the man, and he slept; then he took one of his ribs
and closed up its place with flesh. And the rib that the Lord God had
taken from the man he made into a woman and brought her to the man.
Then the man said,

> *"This at last is bone of my bones*
> *and flesh of my flesh;*
> *this one shall be called Woman,*
> *for out of Man this one was taken."*

Therefore a man leaves his father and his mother and clings to his wife,
and they become one flesh. And the man and his wife were both naked,
and were not ashamed.

Genesis 2:18, 21-25

An elderly couple lay down for bed one night. The woman said to her husband, "When we were younger, you used to lie close to me." The man sighed and moved closer.

The woman said, "I remember when you used to hold my hand." The man sighed again, a little frustrated, but reached out and took her hand.

Then the woman said, "I remember when you used to nibble my ear." This time the man angrily threw back the covers and got up to leave. Shocked, the woman asked, "Where are you going?"

The man replied, "To get my teeth!"

I love this story. Simple but moving, it offers a glimpse of a love that can last a lifetime — selfless, sacrificial, the kind love that gets a husband out of his warm bed to find his teeth in the cup of Efferdent so he can bless his wife!

As that husband would probably tell you, one of the most important things about love, marriage, and sexual intimacy is that it's hard work. When we fall in love, it seems so easy. But maintaining love over decades — that's another story. Most couples have seasons when they fall out of love. Most report that their sex life seems boring at times. Most think about calling it quits. Most fight fairly regularly. But those who don't give up, who work on their marriage, who endure "until they are parted by death" find profound rewards. This book is written to help you find or rediscover a love that not only stays but deepens over the years.

The Changing Face of Marriage

The social changes of the past few decades have done nothing to dampen the human need for romantic partnership, for someone with whom to share love and intimacy, but those changes have certainly altered the way relationships play out. Divorce rates have declined since their peak in the 1980s, and yet the probability of divorce for a couple marrying today is still between 40 and 50 percent.[1] What's more, many of the couples whose marriages do last will have serious and painful issues to work through.

Young people who have seen the reality behind those statistics, watching as their parents and grandparents divorced, have decided to postpone their own weddings, so the marriage rate has declined precipitously in the past 50 years. In 1960, 72 percent of all Americans over 18 were married; in 2011, it was 51 percent. In 1960, the average age of men and women marrying for the first time was 22.8 and 20.3, respectively; in 2011, the average age was 28.7 and 26.5[2] I seldom officiate at a wedding where the parents of both the bride and groom are still happily married. Typically at least one set of parents is divorced.

The number of young people choosing to live together rather than marry is dramatically higher as well, and their success rates are even worse than those who marry, with 50 percent breaking up within the first five years.[3] It would appear that whether we're married or cohabiting, we're not sure how to have lasting, loving relationships. And where, at a time when this generation's role models have made such a mess of marriage, would we go to learn about those relationships?

In order to get a driver's license you have to pass a test, and high schools offer driver's education to teach what we all know is essential to safe driving. But a marriage license? To get one in my home state of Kansas, you need just $75 and a birth certificate. There is no training, no preparation, no certification. Some churches, including ours, require premarital counseling, but when you're young, you may not be paying attention because you figure you know it all and love is enough.

The church where my wife LaVon and I got married gave us one hour of premarital counseling with our pastor. *One hour* to prepare a 17-year-old and 18-year-old for a lifetime relationship! There are so many things I wish someone had told us, though I have to admit that we, like most young people, may not have paid attention.

If you haven't had any instruction and then hit turbulence in your marriage, where do you go for help? You can seek out a counselor, but tragically many of us—let's face it, mostly men—tend to think that going to a counselor is a sign that we're failing. So instead we say to our spouses, "Go ahead, you can see a counselor, but I don't need one." Guys, that's like having a car that you love and deciding it's not manly to take it to a mechanic if it overheats. You can keep on driving it, but eventually you'll ruin the engine. In marriage, it's helpful and sometimes essential to consult an objective third party who is trained in helping couples work through common, and sometimes not so common, marital issues.

With so many people struggling in marriage and young people postponing marriage, does it mean that marriage is dead? A lot of people think so. It's not hard to find pundits suggesting that maybe humans just aren't cut out for long-term, monogamous relationships. A Pew Research Center study found that 40 percent of people think marriage is obsolete, though interestingly enough a majority of those respondents still want to get married!

In that study, researchers asked people to characterize their level of happiness and found that, despite all the challenges of marriage, those who were married were 11–28 percent more likely to describe themselves as "very happy" than those who were single.[4]

Of course, those statistics don't mean that being single causes unhappiness; many singles are very happy. What it tells me is that marriage isn't obsolete and that the institution offers something valuable to those who figure out how to make it work. It just looks like more of us need help in figuring that out.

The Meaning and Mission of Marriage

Not long ago I spoke to a young couple in our congregation who told me they wanted to move in together but weren't interested in getting married. They said, "We don't know why we need a piece of paper to love and be committed to one another." Another young man commented how he thought a legal contract for love was silly. In his mind, it was more romantic to love someone who could leave if she wanted. Her choosing to stay showed she wasn't sticking around just because of a piece of paper. His perspective reflected a view held by many young adults today.

Marriage rightly understood is much more than a piece of paper. Christians and Jews believe that marriage was created by God, that it was God's way of addressing a need in human beings. It was part of the very story of Creation, told in the opening pages of the Bible. Some read that story literally, others more poetically or figuratively, but in either case we agree that the story is archetypal and deals with some of the really big questions in life: "Where did we come from?" "Is there a God, and if so, what is God like?" "What does it mean to be human?" and, yes, "What is the meaning and mission of marriage?"

Looking back, I wish I had understood more clearly that marriage has a mission. I was madly in love with LaVon. I couldn't keep my hands off her. But everything else was guesswork. Nobody ever said, "Adam, this is the meaning of marriage. This is your mission statement. This is what you're supposed to do after you say, 'I do.'"

From the first, the Bible makes clear that marriage is a calling from God to care for, bless, and serve another. We are called to channel God's love and kindness to all, but marriage calls us to do it in a special, intentional way toward someone with whom we will partner in life.

In Genesis we find two Creation stories. The first, found in Genesis chapter one, repeatedly states that everything God created was "good." On the seventh day God takes it a step further and declares everything he had made "very good." In the second Creation story, found in Genesis chapter two, we reach the first thing that is "not good."

"It is not good," declares God, "that the man should be alone." This speaks of the hunger each of us is born with for intimacy with others. And so God says, "I will make him a helper as his partner" (Genesis 2:18).

The new and improved model of the human — woman!

God brings to Adam all the animals and birds formed out of the ground. Adam is given the prerogative of naming each and, it seems, the opportunity to find among them a creature who could be a partner and companion. But, says Genesis 2:20b, "no suitable helper was found" (NIV).

God looks at the man and sees the longing in his heart. God says, as I imagine the story, "I have something in mind for you that you would not believe if I were to tell you." God causes the man to fall into a deep sleep and takes from his side a rib. He closes up the place with flesh and forms a new and improved model of the human — woman!

I picture Adam wiping the sleep from his eyes and taking a look at Eve, so like him and yet so mysteriously and maddeningly different. As Adam's heart beat faster, he must have thought, *This is what I have been waiting for!* Genesis 2:23 quotes him as saying,

> *"This at last is bone of my bones*
> *and flesh of my flesh;*
> *this one shall be called Woman,*
> *for out of Man this one was taken."*

The narrator of Genesis continues, "Therefore a man leaves his father and his mother and clings to his wife, and they become one flesh" (v. 24) — a euphemism for sexual intimacy. The narrator goes on to say that "the man and his wife were both naked, and were not ashamed" (v. 25). Right here, in the foundational story of the Bible, we find love, sex, and marriage, presented in such a way as to make clear the meaning and mission inherent in the partnership that brings all three together. The story tells us that marriage is God's gift to men and women, a way of blessing us as it meets a fundamental, existential need we have as human beings. Genesis doesn't talk of romance or emotion, but rather of God's offer of a partner — a companion and helper — with whom to walk through this life.

The mission of marriage is for both husband and wife to be helpers, partners, and companions for one another. Being a helper does not imply a subservient role for either the woman or the man. The word for "helper" in Genesis 2 is the Hebrew *ezer*, always used in the Bible to connote one who is stronger coming to help one who is weaker. In fact, it is often applied to God himself in relation to humanity. The idea is not that a weaker person is brought in to serve the stronger, but that two people bring their mutual strengths to the relationship in order to bless one another.

Both parties in any marriage are intended to be each other's helpers and companions. They are making a covenant with God and with each other to bless and minister to one another. They are meant to be counterparts, to complement each other the way the left shoe complements the right shoe in a long journey on a rocky road. Ideally, it's an equality that comes from complementary strengths working in unison.

To be a helper is to seek the best for the person you're helping—in the way they can best receive it. Some of us need to be reminded that our job is not to solve all the problems our spouse brings to us; in fact, most people hate it when we try to solve all their problems. When they bring us problems and lay out things that are burdening them, the help we can bring is to come alongside them, encourage and bless them, and build them up—the very things we need when we are troubled. That is part of what it means to be a helper.

Eros, Agape, and the Vision of Marriage

When I married LaVon, I made a covenant with God to bless her, to encourage her, and to incarnate ("put flesh on") the love of God for her. I believe I'm called to build her up and help her be the woman God wants her to be, just as part of her job in my life is to help me be the man God wants me to be.

Everything we've talked about and will talk about in the rest of this book shows that these are things we find very hard to do. Part of the reason for the difficulty is built into our very complementarity—in so many ways, those who marry are very, very different from each other. We think differently. We experience things differently. We see the world differently. The things I think are going to bless LaVon sometimes only irritate her. Any man who's ever bought a woman a vacuum cleaner for Christmas—and I have to admit I've done it—knows what I'm talking about.

Men and women may have had difficulties understanding each other's needs from the very beginning. In the Genesis story, when God confronts Adam about eating the forbidden fruit, Adam instantly blames Eve. Reading that passage makes me smile, because this is precisely how marriages work!

We still carry the differences that can drive each other crazy, but at least we've been given the blueprints for how to treat each other.

When Eve was created, she may have looked at Adam and then at God and said, "Really? Him? This is the best you could do? He burps, he scratches, he never listens to me, and he watches the animals play games all weekend long! When he does pay attention to me, he can't keep his hands to himself! And did you see what he made me for my birthday last year? A broom!"

Adam may have countered by saying, "Do you know how crazy she makes me? She's moody. She's always after me to pick up my things. And the talking! How could one person have so many things to say? She doesn't give me any time just to kick back in my man cave. And when it comes to 'be fruitful and multiply,' I'm not sure she got the message!"

We still carry the differences that can drive each other crazy, but at least we've been given the blueprints for how to treat each other. What the Hebrew word *ezer* (helper) is to our Old Testament understanding of marriage, *agape* is to our New

Testament understanding. *Agape* is of course the Greek word for "love," or more precisely one of the Greek words for love. Another word, *eros*, has to do with the passionate, sexual side of love — we get the word *erotic* from it. Eros is also the name of the Greek god whose Roman counterpart was Cupid; Cupid's arrow was said to produce the heart-pounding desire that kicks off the passionate early days of romantic longing.

But you can't build a marriage or a long-term relationship on *eros* alone. It's just not possible. Eventually, *eros* must be transformed into something more substantial. Augmented by the desire to help and encourage, to nurture and lift up, *eros* is transformed into *agape*, a selfless, sacrificial love that wishes the best for the other.

Agape, which is independent of our own personal feelings, is what God intended for us from the time he created us. Paul describes that love in his famous passage from 1 Corinthians, where he writes, "Love is patient; love is kind; love is not envious or boastful or arrogant or rude. It does not insist on its own way; it is not irritable or resentful; it does not rejoice in wrongdoing, but rejoices in the truth. It bears all things, believes all things, hopes all things, endures all things. Love never ends" (1 Corinthians 13:4-8).

Jesus taught and championed this beautiful ideal. He said it was what God seeks from each of us. Jesus, at the end of his life, showed us what that love looks like. As he hung on the cross, he was saying, in effect, "This is *agape* — laying down your life for others."

Jesus showed us the ideal, the pattern for what love looks like. It's what we're called to strive for in all our relationships, but especially in marriage. Paul writes, "Husbands, love your wives, just as Christ loved the church and gave himself up for her" (Ephesians 5:25).

It is a lovely thought. Unfortunately, men and women do not readily display *agape* love toward each other. By nature, I am not selfless but selfish. It is easy to believe that the world revolves around me. I don't automatically think first of others. But as a Christian, I hear the call of Jesus to love LaVon selflessly and sacrificially, regardless of what I'm feeling or what my inclinations are. Christ's very life was *agape* love writ large, and I decided many years ago to follow him. *Agape* is what I'm aiming for. It's what I pray that I might demonstrate more of, both to LaVon and to others.

As we strive to live the Christian ideal, the Holy Spirit changes our hearts in a process called conversion. We are changed from the inside out, so that over the course of a lifetime we're meant to become more and more loving. In twenty years I should be able to love LaVon more fully, selflessly, and completely than I do now. The biblical and theological word for this process is sanctification, or being perfected in love by God.

There are certain practices that seem to help me become more loving. I feel closest to God when I've been praying, worshiping, and studying Scripture, and when I am doing these things I'm also a far better husband. I think less of myself, and it becomes almost second nature to think of LaVon. Conversely, when I drift away from God (yes, preachers drift away from God), I tend to become more impatient and irritable, thinking more about myself and what LaVon is not doing for me.

Our capacity to fulfill the mission of marriage is strengthened by our faith in Christ and our desire to serve him, and by the work of the Holy Spirit as we grow in faith.

To understand the mission of marriage, it is helpful to have a vision of what that mission looks like when we actually fulfill it—to have a "preferred picture of the future" for our marriage.

"Across the course of our love and our life together, you've made me a better person."

So, what does it look like when we live out this mission? What is the vision? My parents and LaVon's parents both divorced; like so many others, we didn't see the vision lived out by our parents. But as a pastor, I have been able to witness this kind of love many times. I see it when I officiate at the renewal of wedding vows by a couple celebrating their fiftieth anniversary, or when I speak with a husband or wife who has just lost a spouse after a long marriage. I let them paint the picture for me, and I find my vision for LaVon and me strengthened.

Sometimes I get glimpses of the vision from the briefest of comments. Not long ago, I watched the end come for a man in our congregation who had been married for many years. His wife was with him in the care center just before he passed away, and before she left for the day he looked at her and said, "I want you to know this: Across the course of our love and our life together, you've made me a better person."

It was a remarkable testimony of the power of love and of the ministry and mission of marriage. His words reminded me that LaVon has made me a better person, and my hope and prayer is that, should I die before she does, she might say, "You know, over the course of our years together, Adam made me a better person."

There are times when the vision is shown to me in profound and deeply moving ways. The most powerful vision I've seen in my ministry of what marriage is meant to look like is the story of John and Denise.

John and Denise were among the founding members of our church. They and their two elementary-age sons helped in a host of ways as we launched our community of believers.

Denise had suffered a brain tumor many years earlier, but it had long been in remission. Then, about three or four years after the founding of our church, the tumor returned. John and Denise learned that it was cancerous and inoperable, and though the doctor tried to slow its progress, the tumor would not respond to treatment. It was obvious that at some point before too long, she would succumb.

John, Denise, and their sons moved to Columbia, Missouri, to be closer to family. One day several years after they had moved, John called to let me know the end was drawing near. I drove the two hours to Columbia in order to spend some time with them. I rang the doorbell and heard John shout from the top of the stairs, "Adam, it's unlocked. Come on in."

He had just finished giving Denise a bath and was doing her hair and putting on her makeup. I watched as he took her in his arms, carried her downstairs, and set her gently at the kitchen table. He made us bologna sandwiches, and gently fed Denise, wiping her face tenderly after each bite. Now and then Denise would have a brief flash of awareness, as though she recognized something familiar, but most of the time there was a blank look in her eyes. When we finished, John and I prayed together for Denise, giving her to God.

As I got in my car to start back, I broke down. The tears flowed down my face. *This,* I thought, *is what marriage looks like.* It wasn't about a piece of paper. It had long ago stopped being about sex or romance, fun, or even friendship. This was marital love, a commitment that John and Denise had made, for better or worse, for richer or poorer, in sickness and in health, to love and cherish one another until they were parted by death.

This is *agape,* and it's something profound, holy, and beautiful. This is God's mission and vision for marriage.

REFLECT AND ENGAGE

Wedding Vows Review

They say that you shouldn't sign any document without a lawyer present and a thorough understanding of what you're agreeing to. That may be the case when you are buying a house or car, or taking out a loan, but it's really the opposite in the covenant of marriage. There's no way to fully understand what you're getting into until you've experienced it. You sign on the dotted line first, and only over time do you understand what it really means. If you had any idea what marriage would really look like ahead of time, you might not agree to it at all!

The vows you make are necessarily vague because the meaning of those commitments evolve over time, just as you evolve and change as people. Your spouse will not be the same person on your twentieth anniversary as on the day you married. And neither will you! Because both of you will change over time, what you both need in order to be loved, honored, and cherished will also change over time.

Take time together to think about the vows you made when you married. Begin by finding a copy of your wedding vows, whether you wrote your own or used traditional wording. Take a moment to reflect on them privately, and then discuss the following questions.

- Why did you choose these words at the time you married? What did they mean to you at that time?
- What promise has proven most challenging over the years?

Did you expect keeping it to be difficult, or has that come as a surprise?

- What do those vows mean to you today? Are there elements that mean something different to you now than they did when you married?

- Separately, write new vows to one another that reflect your current understanding of marriage and the unique strengths and challenges of your relationship. Come back together to discuss what you wrote. How are these vows different from the ones you said at your wedding?

Pray Together

Make time each day to pray as a couple. Whether you use a written prayer like the one below, speak in your own words, or pray silently while holding hands, seeking God together can bring you closer and invite God's influence into your relationship.

Dear God, we know that we do not fully understand what it means to love one another unconditionally, but we know that you do. Help our marriage to embody the kind of love you have for us. Give us the courage and humility to seek forgiveness when we need it, and to recommit ourselves to one another and to you daily. Amen.

On Your Own

Every morning, read the new vows you wrote and think about how you can fulfill those promises that day. Remember the elderly man who said his wife had "made him a better person"? Ask yourself what you would want your spouse to say about you toward the end of your life. Are your words and actions today contributing to making you the spouse you want to be? What might you need to do differently in order to be a better spouse?

If You're Single

You don't magically become a new person as soon as you slip a ring on your finger. The character and values you bring into marriage are developed over many years and continue developing alongside your partner. Think about the type of spouse you want to be. Write down the vows you could imagine making to your future spouse. What promises might be most challenging for you?

2

WHAT SHE WANTS, WHAT HE WANTS

If then there is any encouragement in Christ, any consolation from love, any sharing in the Spirit, any compassion and sympathy, make my joy complete: be of the same mind, having the same love, being in full accord and of one mind. Do nothing from selfish ambition or conceit, but in humility regard others as better than yourselves. Let each of you look not to your own interests, but to the interests of others. Let the same mind be in you that was in Christ Jesus.

Philippians 2:1-5

"One day," a member of our church told me, "my housework-challenged husband decided to wash his sweatshirt. Seconds after he stepped into the laundry room, he shouted to me, 'What setting should I use on the washing machine?' 'It depends,' I replied. 'What does it say on your shirt?' He yelled back, 'Ohio State!'"

Men and women have different needs, different ways of giving and receiving love, and different ways of communicating, even when they think they want the same thing. We explored some of these differences in a Love, Sex, and Marriage survey that we conducted in late 2011. The survey was taken by 5,184 people, both single and married, who told us about their love lives. This anonymous online survey was taken by members of the church I pastor, The United Methodist Church of the Resurrection in Leawood, Kansas, and also by people from across the country, including persons with no religious affiliation. Methodology and results were verified and confirmed by Hanover Research in Washington, D.C. Though the results reflect information only from those who took the survey, they give a glimpse of broad trends in marriage and dating relationships. Throughout the book we'll draw from this honest look at the state of relationships, including the blessings and frustrations of marriages and dating relationships among people of all ages.

The survey results showed notable differences between men and women, and between people of various ages and stages in life. The results also help us draw some conclusions about what works and doesn't work in building lasting relationships. In this chapter we'll consider what the survey tells us about how the needs and desires of men and women differ and how those needs change over the course of a lifetime. We'll learn about what men and women say they need from their partners or mates.

Understanding What Men and Women Want in a Mate

Marriage, as we have seen, is a covenant relationship in which two people promise, first to God and then to each other, to demonstrate love, offer help, and befriend one another. We are meant to bless, build up, encourage, and even heal one another. This calls for a selfless love that is not dependent upon feelings and is expressed through actions.

It's almost as if we speak different languages.

With this in mind, let's take a look at our survey. In studying the responses, it's clear that men and women have different ways of giving and receiving love and that sometimes, even when we think we want the same thing, we actually mean two different things. It's almost as if we speak different languages, or perhaps different dialects of the same language.

We'll begin with the nearly 1,000 single people who participated in our survey. More than 80 percent of that group said they hoped to be married someday, so we asked them for the key qualities they were seeking in a potential mate.

The single most important attribute, according to single men 19 to 49, was honesty and trustworthiness. Second, they wanted a woman of strong faith. (It's worth keeping in mind here that many of the respondents were people of faith themselves, so we might expect this result to be different in a survey of the general population.) Third, they wanted someone who was physically attractive. Fourth, they were seeking a woman with intelligence. And fifth, they wanted a woman who was fun or humorous, someone with whom they could laugh and have a good time.

Single Men 19–49
1. Honest/trustworthy
2. Strong faith
3. Attractive
4. Intelligent
5. Fun/humorous

Single men aged 50 and older (the oldest man in our survey was 95) had a somewhat different list. The attribute they told us they valued most was attractiveness, although men over age 70 cited intelligence first. They rated honesty and trustworthiness the second most important quality. Third was emotional stability, a quality that didn't make the top five for the younger men. Fourth was a strong faith, and fifth, as with the younger men, was a sense of fun and humor.

Single Men 50–90+
1. Attractive or intelligent (over age 70)
2. Honest/trustworthy
3. Emotionally stable
4. Strong faith
5. Fun/humorous

Each of us may put a different spin on those lists, but there's one attribute I'll focus on for a moment. As the results of the survey came in, I went on my Facebook page and asked the men what it meant to them for a woman to be physically attractive. One of the guys said, "She doesn't need to look like a model and she doesn't have to be a size two. In fact, when I see a woman who looks like that I want to say, 'Eat a sandwich, lady!' She just needs to look healthy and like she has given some thought to her appearance — not like she has raccoons living in her hair!"

Others concurred that it's not a particular shape or size that determines whether a woman is physically attractive. It's the whole package — how she dresses, how she carries herself, how she does her hair, the way she talks and maintains eye contact, and her overall personality. And the mix changes over time. What is physically attractive to a young man at 16 is different from what he finds appealing at 46. Still, there's no getting around the fact that men are visual creatures. As one respondent put it, "We kind of have a thing about curb appeal."

Now let's look at what the single women said they were looking for in a potential mate. For single women age 19 to 49, the number-one attribute was the same one sought by the men in their age group: they wanted a man who was honest and trustworthy. Number two was a man who was funny, who could make them laugh. Third, they wanted someone with a strong faith. For the fourth item on the list, there was disagreement by age, with women in their 20s naming intelligence while women in their 30s and 40s listed emotional stability. Rounding out the list at number five was a man who was a good communicator.

Single Women 19–49

1. Honest/trustworthy
2. Fun/humorous
3. Strong faith
4. Intelligent or emotionally stable
5. Good communicator

The list varied a bit for women age 50 and up, with trustworthiness at the top, a strong faith second, emotional stability third, and good communication skills fourth. Number five differed by age, with women up to age 69 listing a sense of humor, and women age 70 and above listing compassion.

Single Women 50–90+

1. Honest/trustworthy
2. Strong faith
3. Emotionally stable
4. Good communicator
5. Fun/humorous or compassionate

It's worth noting that neither group of women listed "physically attractive" as one of the top five attributes they look for in a man. This is good news for many men! The women valued a man's ability to communicate over his outward appearance. (Based on the women's comments, they, like their male counterparts, did care about appearance and seemed most interested in men who took care of themselves and paid attention to grooming and looking nice.) We should also mention that every age group of women over 30 was looking for a man who was emotionally stable. So, other than attractiveness, women and men listed the same basic attributes they were looking for, although in a slightly different order.

If LaVon and I weren't married, I would want to be the kind of man she would fall in love with.

If we are seeking to bless the other person in a marriage relationship, these lists give us a pretty good indication of what attributes men and women value in their mates or potential mates.

As I looked over those results, I thought about the fact that if LaVon and I weren't married, I would want to be the kind of man she would fall in love with. It has been said that it's more important to *be* the right person than to find the right person. The Bible, too, teaches us the importance of being the right person — of putting the other person's needs above our own.

Once we know what our spouses or potential spouses want, there are two things that get in the way: By nature we find it easy to be self-centered, thinking first about ourselves and our own needs and wants; and even when we do want to bless the other person, we don't always know how to do it.

Although I try not to be, I'm quite aware most of the time of what I need and what I want. However, I have to work at thinking about what LaVon needs and wants. It is Jesus Christ who modeled for us what it means to practice selfless love and to lead a selfless life. He gave us the ultimate demonstration in his death on the cross. As we follow him, we invite God's Holy Spirit to change us from the inside out, so that we become more conscious of the needs of others. The closer we draw to God — the more we worship, pray, study, and grow — the more we are able to love selflessly.

Paul describes how we are called to live: "Do nothing from selfish ambition or conceit, but in humility regard others as better than yourselves. Let each of you look not to your own interests, but to the interests of others. Let the same mind be in you that was in Christ Jesus" (Philippians 2:3-5).

Growth toward that ideal is part of what it means to be a spiritually mature Christian. As we grow, we must strive to understand what constitutes love for the other person, keeping in mind that men and women experience love and its blessings in different ways. This means sometimes the things LaVon does for me that make me feel loved and blessed are not the things I should be doing for her, since her needs may be different from my own.

Love Languages, Love Tanks, and Love Banks

There are several metaphors that can be helpful in thinking about the importance of blessing and caring for one another, as well as actually doing it. The first metaphor comes from *The Five Love Languages*, a wildly successful 1992 book by author, speaker, and counselor Gary Chapman.[5] In the book, Chapman describes five primary "love languages," or ways in which people receive and give love. The five love languages are words of affirmation, quality time, receiving gifts, acts of service, and physical touch.

Do unto others as they would have us do unto them.

Chapman notes that all of us have primary and secondary love languages and that a man's and a woman's primary love languages are hardly ever the same. In my case, my natural inclination is to give love in the same way I like to receive it, in essence following the Golden Rule — *do unto others as I'd have them do unto me.* But when it comes to marriage, what we really have to figure out is how to do unto others as they would have us do unto them. I need to give love to LaVon in the way that makes her feel loved, not in the way that makes me feel loved.

To see how this plays out in our lives, LaVon and I went to one of Gary Chapman's websites, www.5lovelanguages.com,[6] and took a quiz designed to pinpoint our primary and secondary love languages. The quiz is a means of helping couples understand how best to give love to one another. In fact, it is not just for romantic partners; it can provide great information in any relationship.

My primary love language turns out to be words of affirmation. That makes sense. When LaVon says to me, "I'm so proud of you and proud to be your wife, and I think what you just did was great," it makes me feel loved and valued. I want to make my wife proud, and when she tells me she's proud of me, I feel very close to her.

In contrast, LaVon's primary love language is quality time. It's not that she doesn't like words of affirmation, but that's not the primary way she experiences love. Yet, because my primary love language is receiving words of affirmation, it tends to be the way I express love to her. When I tell her, "You look beautiful" or "I'm so proud of what you did," she appreciates it, but it doesn't make up for the times, night after night, when I'm late coming home from church meetings. To her, my actions speak louder than words, and the message is clear: Adam loves the church more than he loves me. That's just one example of why it's so important for us to understand each other's love languages and to give love in the way the other person best receives it.

Chapman uses a second metaphor in his book. He writes about the spouse's emotional "love tank." That got me thinking of the gas tank in my car. A big, beautiful car with the world's most powerful engine isn't going anywhere if the fuel tank is empty, and it's worth remembering that different cars require different kinds of fuel. If you have a diesel engine and put regular fuel in the tank, you may damage the engine. It's also important to note that, just as a car uses fuel and requires regular fill-ups, relationships use emotional energy and need regular filling of our emotional fuel tanks.

Have you ever run out of gas in a car? I have on several occasions. I always think I can go just a little farther even when the fuel light is on. Then suddenly, the car begins to miss, the power steering goes, and the car coasts to a stop. It's a terrible feeling when you know you'll have to hoof it to a gas station and bring back fuel to start the car again. Something very similar can happen in a relationship when your partner's love tank is empty.

You forget to fill up the love tank.

Filling your loved one's tank comes naturally in the beginning. When you start to date, you're attentive, you're complimentary, you're generous with gifts, and you're eager to make your loved one smile and feel appreciated. I've officiated at over three hundred weddings, and during the counseling sessions I always ask the couple, "How did you meet? How did you fall in love?" The women often say, "Oh, it was great. That first night we stayed up and talked for hours. It was just awesome!" I'm sometimes tempted to say, "I hope you enjoyed it, because that's the last time it's going to happen!"

Our Love, Sex and Marriage survey asked people how much quality time they spent talking to their mates every day. The results are shown in the graph on the next page.

As you can see, the largest group of respondents spent from fifteen to thirty minutes a day, and a significant number spent less than fifteen minutes. That's a far cry from those early, six-hour conversations. And within a few years of marriage the flowers, heartfelt compliments, and nights on the town give way to the everyday stuff of life: paying the bills, caring for the kids, and pursuing careers. You forget to fill up the love tank. And now and then you cause conflict, say something insensitive, or do something hurtful, and the tank is drained even more rapidly. If you're not working diligently to refill that tank, at some point it's going to wind up empty. You'll look up and find that your once-happy household has broken down and run out of gas and is sitting on the side of the road.

The bottom line? Keep filling that tank!

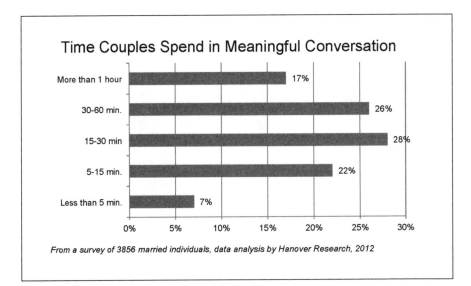

Time Couples Spend in Meaningful Conversation

More than 1 hour	17%
30-60 min.	26%
15-30 min	28%
5-15 min.	22%
Less than 5 min.	7%

From a survey of 3856 married individuals, data analysis by Hanover Research, 2012

The third metaphor I find helpful in understanding our partner's needs and seeking to meet them comes from Barbara De Angelis and Willard F. Harley Jr., both marriage counselors. They write about our partner's heart as a "love bank."[7] We make deposits when we do something that blesses, encourages, or lifts up the other person; we make withdrawals when we take emotional energy from them. When you are dating, you are constantly making deposits. Each phone call, text, or card with kind words is a deposit. Flowers? A deposit. A romantic date? Deposit. Sharing your feelings? Deposit. Listening, kissing, holding hands, snuggling, going to see those movies you hate? All deposits. By the time you get married, you've got quite an account balance.

Then you settle into the routine of married life, and you expect your mate to do certain things for you. No problem, but each one is a withdrawal. Living together, you find you irritate one another from time to time. More withdrawals. He wants intimacy. Withdrawal. She doesn't want to be intimate. Withdrawal. Hurtful words, too tired to talk, forget an important date — withdrawal, withdrawal, withdrawal.

At some point the account balance you'd built up while dating is gone. You're making more withdrawals than deposits. Then one day you get a notice of insufficient funds. Our kids could always tell when mommy was not happy with daddy. She sent notices for insufficient funds in the form of a look that was unmistakable. The kids said it was like lightning coming out of her eyes. And they could tell when I was upset with her, because my jaw would clench and I'd get really quiet and storm off into the other room. They knew one of us had made a withdrawal bigger than the credit balance in the account.

In looking at my own life and the lives of those I've counseled over the years, it's clear that in marriage relationships we often allow the other person to go on overdraft status for a long time, sometimes for years. It's also clear that that's a costly practice. At some point you pass the "insufficient funds" stage, and you get a notice that says "account closed." We refer to those notices as divorce papers, and they come when the other person says, "I'm empty. I have nothing left inside." That's how important the routine deposits into our mates' love banks are, and how important it is to know the kind of deposits that meet their needs.

If we're not speaking the same love language, or if the language is right but the dialect is off, we might have the best intentions in the world and still wind up getting no credit at all for our deposit. In fact, if our love language is far enough off, our deposit could actually count as a withdrawal, as when a well-intentioned but clueless husband — yes, me again — uses Christmas to give a vacuum cleaner or something equally romantic.

We asked the men and women who took our Love, Sex, and Marriage survey, "What are the things your spouse does that make you feel closest to him or her?" In other words, what constitutes a deposit in your love bank? We provided a list, from which respondents could pick as many items as they wanted. Here are the answers given by the 1,479 married men, broken down by age groups:

Married Men 19–29
1. Having fun with me
2. Demonstrations of affection
3. Sexual intimacy
4. Words of admiration/compliments
5. Sharing feelings with me

Married Men 30–49

1. Sexual intimacy

2. Demonstrations of affection

3. Having fun with me

4. Words of admiration/compliments

5. Listening to me

Married Men 50–69

1. Having fun with me

2. Demonstrations of affection

3. Sharing feelings with me

4. Listening to me

5. Sexual intimacy

Married Men 70–100

1. Sharing feelings

2. Tender touch/affection

3. Listening to me

4. Having fun with me

5. Words of admiration/compliments

It's worth noting that although sexual intimacy didn't make the top five for married men 70–100, it didn't drop off the radar altogether. It was sixth.

We then asked the men a followup question, "If you could only pick one of these answers, which would be the single most important thing you'd want to hold onto, the one that makes you feel closest to your partner?" Interestingly enough, sexual

intimacy was not the answer in any age group. The number-
one answer involved demonstrations of affection, something
that rings true with me. When LaVon puts her arm around me
or takes my hand or snuggles up close to me, that's far more
important than anything else she does to make me feel loved.
The notion that guys aren't interested in nonsexual intimate
touch just isn't true.

Now let's turn to the answers given us by the 2,222 married
women who responded to our survey.

Married Women 19–29

1. Sharing his feelings with me
2. Having fun with me
3. Demonstrations of affection
4. Listening to me
5. Words of admiration/compliments

Married Women 30–49

1. Sharing his feelings with me
2. Having fun with me
3. Listening to me
4. Demonstrations of affection
5. When he cares for the children

Married Women 50–69

1. Sharing his feelings with me
2. Having fun with me
3. Demonstrations of affection
4. Listening to me
5. Makes me feel safe and secure

Married Women 70–100

1. Demonstrations of affection
2. Sharing his feelings with me
3. Words of admiration/compliments
4. Tender touch
5. When he worships with me

It's interesting that the men's and women's lists were very similar except for sexual intimacy, which generally ranked in the top five for men but not for women. Surprisingly, "sharing his or her feelings with me" was on both sets of lists. This was especially puzzling because as I checked the surveys, I saw women complaining a lot about men not sharing their feelings.

"Put your gadgets down, turn them off, look me in the eye, and show me you care."

It struck me that the same words must mean something different to women and men. When I followed up on Facebook, asking men and women what they meant, the women said: "Sharing your feelings with me is not grunting. I need you to tell me more. I want details. I want information. I want you to tell me what you were thinking and what you were feeling." For the guys, it was much simpler: "Tell me exactly what happened, and give it to me in sixty seconds or less." In addition, guys tend to think we can listen to women share their feelings while we're doing something else. But women said, "Put your gadgets down, turn them off, look me in the eye, and show me you care. Don't pretend you're paying attention." In this case, getting it wrong means it's not a deposit; it's a withdrawal.

Investing in Your Marriage

Most of us routinely sacrifice to invest for retirement. We'll choose not to do something today so we can make sure we have resources available later. Let me encourage you to think about deposits in the love bank as investments in the long-term health of your marriage, which ultimately will result in greater long-term happiness and satisfaction in life. Look at these deposits as choosing to do things you might not otherwise do because they're going to bless the other person. And here's a tip: When you're doing these things, you're not making a deposit if you say, "I'll do this with you, but I really hate it." It's a deposit when you say, "You know, if you like to do that, it sounds great. Let's do it together." Don't complain the whole time, and don't make a big deal out of it. Eventually you'll come to enjoy these activities simply because they bless the other person. Think of them as long-term investments.

We make payments by giving our time and love in ways that can be received and valued by the other person. We seek to bless, minister to, build up, and work to achieve the best for the other. That is what the apostle Paul meant when he wrote, "Let each of you look not to your own interests, but to the interests of others. Let the same mind be in you that was in Christ Jesus" (Philippians 2:4-5). Instead of seeking to benefit ourselves, we choose to think first about the interests of the other and to ask ourselves, *How can I bless you?* Investments in our partner's love bank give our lives a kind of rhythm, as we grow in Christ and move from selfishness and into selflessness.

Establishing that kind of rhythm is not easy. It requires courage. It takes intentionality and hard work. Without those things, relationships will suffer. Great marriages involve both partners constantly thinking about how to bless the other, asking, *How can I do this better? How can I improve?* We learn to do the things we might not otherwise be willing to do because it's our mission to bless, build up, and encourage.

In the midst of doing those things, we fall back in love.

Over time, this approach only works when both partners practice it. If one is giving and putting the other first while the other is taking and taking, the situation is unhealthy for both partners. The giving partner is contributing to the other's narcissism and will soon find his or her own love bank empty. If neither partner is giving selflessly, both will quickly come to resent each other. But when both are humbly considering the other partner to be of greater importance, looking first not to their own interests but to the other's, something truly beautiful emerges. I invite you to bring such beauty into your own life by sharing this as your vision for a blessed marriage.

During our thirty years of marriage, there have been times when neither LaVon nor I was making deposits in the other's love bank. There were seasons when we forgot the mission of marriage. In fact, I still experience moments when I see the "insufficient funds" notice in her eyes. When that happens, I wonder, *Are we going to make it? Are we going to pull this out and make it work for the rest of our lives?*

At some point, though, we remember the mission and meaning of marriage, and once again we try to speak each other's love language. We work to refill each other's love tank. We do what we don't always feel like doing, because we know it will bless our beloved. And in the midst of doing those things, we fall back in love.

My hope and prayer is that you will use these metaphors, these simple tools, to rediscover meaning and mission, and to rekindle the love in your relationship.

REFLECT AND ENGAGE

Love Bank Wish List

We have chances every day to respond to our spouse's needs, but sometimes we don't pick up on the clues and hints. Assessments like the one mentioned in the chapter (www.5lovelanguages.com) can help us understand why our spouse might value certain gestures differently than we do because his or her "love language" is different from our own.

Take a few minutes for each of you to make your own list of five specific things your spouse could do that would make you feel loved. Don't be afraid to dream big. Even if "take me to Hawaii" isn't financially possible right now, that wish can give insight into your love language, and you can find another way to relax and spend quality time together.

Once you've written your lists, come back together to share what you've written. Don't be accusatory, lamenting that your partner hasn't already done what you are wishing for (recently or ever). Look at this as a fun opportunity to dream together about ways to bless one another and grow closer as a couple. After reading your lists aloud, discuss the following questions:

- What trends do you notice in each list? Is there a certain "love language" that appears over and over?
- Does anything surprise you about your own list or your spouse's? What insight does this give you about your needs or your spouse's needs?

- Which of the activities listed would be easy to do in the near future? Make plans right now to do one of the items on each list. Keep your spouse's list, and try to make other wishes come true as well.

Pray Together

Dear God, thank you for the opportunities we have every day to show love to one another. Help us to learn what best speaks love to one another and to do those things selflessly. Let your love for us be shown in the way we love one another. Amen.

On Your Own

Think about the insights you and your spouse gained through the writing and sharing of your wish lists. Use these clues to guide you in making small, everyday gestures to show love to your partner. The gestures don't have to be elaborate—just a squeeze of the shoulder for someone who loves touch, or a five-minute period of uninterrupted conversation for someone who cherishes quality time with you.

If You're Single

What makes you feel loved? What gestures—whether from a friend, parent, sibling, or significant other—lift you up and put a smile on your face? A nice compliment? A tight hug? A surprise gift? These are the same things you will crave from your spouse.

Knowing your own needs and being able to express them will save your future spouse a lot of guesswork. Try to figure out the love languages of your close family and friends, to show them love the way they will best feel it.

3

THE SIGNIFICANCE
OF SEXUAL INTIMACY

The husband should give to his wife her conjugal rights, and likewise the wife to her husband. For the wife does not have authority over her own body, but the husband does; likewise the husband does not have authority over his own body, but the wife does. Do not deprive one another except perhaps by agreement for a set time, to devote yourselves to prayer, and then come together again, so that Satan may not tempt you because of your lack of self-control.

1 Corinthians 7:3-5

Recently one of our church members sent me the following note: "On the way back from a Cub Scout meeting, my grandson innocently said to my son, 'Dad, I know babies come from mommies' tummies, but how do they get there in the first place?' After my son hemmed and hawed for awhile, my grandson finally spoke up in disgust: 'You don't have to make up something, Dad. It's okay if you don't know the answer.'"

Well, most of us know the answer, but sometimes we find it uncomfortable to talk about. When Rebecca, our youngest, was ten, she had been learning where babies come from. She asked me, "Dad, you and Mom never did that, did you?" I answered, "How do you think you got here, Becca?" She looked at me with surprise. Then I smiled and told her, "But don't worry. After you were born, we decided we'd never do that again!"

My point, of course, is not simply that it's hard to talk to our children about sexuality. Most couples find it difficult, at least at times, to talk about sexual intimacy with each other, much less to develop a fulfilling intimate relationship. Though physical intimacy plays an important and wonderful role in healthy marital relationships, it can also be a source of tremendous frustration and pain.

As we turn our attention to the subject of sexual intimacy, my hope is to summarize for you what the Bible teaches about the meaning of sex; to talk frankly about what we learned from the 5,184 people who took the sexual intimacy portion of our Love, Sex, and Marriage survey; and finally to offer some hints for improving your intimate life.

Sexual Intimacy in the Bible

We are bombarded with sex. It's all around us, on TV and radio, at the movies, in our magazines, on billboards, and on our computers. One of the few places we feel uncomfortable with sex is in the church. And that's tragic. We've allowed society to dictate what sex is and what it means, and consequently sexual intimacy has lost much of its beauty, power, and significance for far too many people. The Bible speaks regularly about sexual intimacy—not just prohibiting certain things, but positively portraying intimacy as a gift from God.

The Bible's first mention of sex is near the very beginning of the text, in the second chapter of Genesis. Genesis 2 describes the Bible's first marriage—the relationship between Adam and Eve—and at the end of the story, the text says that a man and woman shall cling together and "become one flesh." It goes on to say they "were both naked and were not ashamed" (vv. 24-25).

The text is clearly referring to sexual intimacy, as the man and woman are described in a sexually intimate embrace, and it is just as clearly telling us that sex is not tawdry or something we shouldn't acknowledge or talk about. It is as much a part of God's good creation as anything else mentioned in the story.

In Genesis 2 and throughout the Bible, there are three big ideas when it comes to the purpose and meaning of sexual intimacy. The first involves simple biology: sexual intimacy is the means God devised for human beings to reproduce. It is therefore a means of co-creation with God. In the time before the advent of birth control, any time a man and woman came together in a sexual embrace there was the possibility of creating a new human being. That possibility imbued the sexual act with holiness; it made the act something awesome, powerful, and mysterious all at the same time.

Of course, not everyone who becomes sexually intimate plans to have children, and some people are unable to have children. So procreation is not the only reason for sexual intimacy, but we need to acknowledge that it is one of the reasons. We also need to recognize that God made this act of co-creation pleasurable, almost irresistible, so that we would continue to perpetuate the species, to "be fruitful and multiply" despite the many hardships and sacrifices that go with parenting.

The second idea presented in the Bible regarding physical intimacy is expressed in Genesis, when we read that the man and woman "become one flesh" (v. 24). Sexual intimacy binds our bodies together in an embrace meant to create an emotional bond that deepens our love and affection for one another.

This trivialization of sex, far from liberating us, robs sexual intimacy of its power.

Biologists have studied monogamous mammals, trying to understand the bonding that takes place, and they have found that for some mammals, two hormones are released in the midst of the sexual act that serve to bind the participants together. One is oxytocin, the "cuddle" or "love" hormone, the same hormone that is released when a woman is giving birth and nursing a child. During and after sexual intimacy, this hormone seems to create a feeling of well-being, closeness, security, and love. The other hormone is vasopressin, which also serves, among other things, a bonding role in mammals.

Finally, the Bible presents the concept of sex as a means of one human being knowing another human being more deeply. It is a concept introduced very early in Genesis, which uses the word *know* as a euphemism for sex: "Now the man knew his wife Eve, and she conceived and bore Cain."

In Hebrew, the word for "to know" (and hence the euphemism for sex) is *yada*. I'm not sure if the makers of the television show *Seinfeld* were thinking about this double entendre when they popularized the phrase "yada, yada, yada," but in Scripture the word is a Hebrew euphemism for sexual intimacy. However, its meaning goes far beyond that. In sexual intercourse you become vulnerable, completely open, *naked* before the other. This is meant to be a beautiful thing, holy and profound.

The Trivialization of Sex

Churches don't often spend a lot of time reminding people of the beauty and importance of the sexual act. Conversely, society tends to trivialize and cheapen it. People talk about "hooking up" or having "friends with benefits." From that perspective, sex becomes not the culmination of a deep, meaningful relationship, but instead merely an end in itself. It has become commonplace in our society to think that after a first or second date, a couple might sleep together.

This trivialization of sex, far from liberating us, robs sexual intimacy of its power. We're simply not ready to reveal our innermost selves to another human being after one or two dates; the bonding that happens is premature. And when we pull away from one person and bond quickly with another and another, sexual intimacy eventually no longer bonds us, biochemically or emotionally, to our partner.

To illustrate this I've often used duct tape, that magical all-purpose stuff that will hold most anything together. Casual sexual encounters with multiple partners is like sticking duct tape to something, pulling it off, sticking it to something else, and repeating several times. After three or four uses, this magical stuff simply won't stick anymore. Likewise, if we misuse sex it no longer plays a role in bonding at all. The idea of becoming vulnerable, of knowing another and allowing another to know us, means virtually nothing, because we've completely revealed ourselves to so many people.

Sex is meant to have real impact in our lives. If we trivialize it, if it becomes only about pleasure and release, as wonderful as those are, it no longer functions the way sex was intended to function, as something that cements us together. We have defeated one of its most important purposes.

In 1969, at the height of the sexual revolution, existentialist philosopher and psychologist Rollo May wrote a book called *Love and Will*, in which he described the impact of the sexual revolution, with its divorce of sex from love. He wrote:

By using sensuality to hide sensitivity, we have emasculated sex and left it vapid and empty…. The plethora of books on sex and love…have one thing in common—they oversimplify love and sex, treating the topic like a combination of learning to play tennis and buying life insurance. In this process, we have robbed sex of its power…. The more we became preoccupied with sex, the more truncated and shrunken became the human experience to which it referred.[8]

May's view seems anachronistic and Victorian to many today, and it's certainly true that Western culture has changed dramatically when it comes to sex. But I want at least to lift up the biblical ideal, which states that two people finally become naked and give themselves to one another only after they have made a covenant with God and with each other to love and care for the other until they are parted by death.

Are you a bad person if you've been with someone before you were married? No, you are human.

This biblical ideal seems to have been supported by a study of 2,000 married couples conducted in 2010 and published with an article in *The Journal of Family Psychology*. The study looked at the effect of waiting until after the wedding to have sexual relations. The article said, "Psychologists found that couples who waited until after their wedding night rated the stability of their relationships 22 percent higher than those whose physical relationships developed earlier." It went on to say couples who waited "were also found to have 20 percent increased levels of relationship satisfaction, 12 percent better communication and 15 percent improved 'sexual quality.'"[9]

I understand that many people consider it absurd to wait until after marriage to have sex. But as one who waited and has never slept with another woman aside from LaVon, I find that the biblical ideal has profound meaning in my life. People might ask if I've been missing something after thirty years with one and only one woman, but I can honestly say I feel blessed that the only person who fully knows me and whom I fully know is the woman I married just out of high school. I find something very beautiful about that.

Are you a bad person if you've been with someone before you were married? No, you are human. We long for intimate touch and companionship. It requires extraordinary restraint and self-discipline not to experience sex before marriage. But I do want to lift up this ideal in a world that has forgotten it.

Within this ideal, a beautiful human story unfolds. You make a covenant with another human being, in sickness and in health, no matter what happens: "I am with you. I will love you and remain by your side. When you are old, when you start to sag and wrinkle, when you are not as physically beautiful as you are today, I will be there." Then, after the two of you make this pledge, with your hearts pounding, you see each other naked, you embrace, and you become one flesh. It may be awkward and strange that first time, and you may not get it quite right, but somehow you figure it out together, and the intimate journey begins.

Sex has more meaning than society says it does. I invite you, regardless of whether you have been intimate with another, to reclaim the idea that sex is purposeful and meaningful, and it isn't something to be trivialized.

Having a Good Intimate Life Is Hard Work

Now that we've discussed the ideal, let's look at how it works in real life. Of the 5,184 people who took our Love, Sex, and Marriage survey, 3,856 were married. Based on their answers, the overwhelming impression was that having a satisfying intimate life is hard work. We sometimes imagine that this part of the relationship is going to take care of itself and that everything will come naturally and easily, but it just doesn't work that way. Like any other part of marriage, a satisfying intimate life takes work, for a variety of reasons.

Let's see how this plays out for our group of real-life couples. How satisfied are married people with their intimate relationships? The graph below shows a breakdown, by age, of married respondents who said they were dissatisfied.

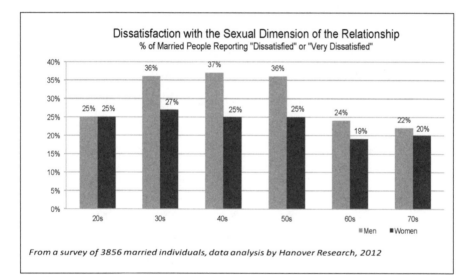

From a survey of 3856 married individuals, data analysis by Hanover Research, 2012

In the comments section, respondents listed some of the reasons they were dissatisfied. Here are some typical responses from the women: Teenagers! We're both too tired. Please, more nonsexual touch. Our love life has become boring. For men, the primary basis of frustration was the desire for more frequency, along with a wish that their mates would initiate or express a desire for them.

Some reasons were given by both men and women. Respondents in their 50s mentioned the impact of menopause or prostate cancer. Those in their 30s and 40s reported that children and work-related stress created diminished intimacy. One man summed it up this way: "We're too pooped to whoop!"

In researching this chapter I read David Snarch's helpful book, *Intimacy and Desire*.[10] Snarch, a sex therapist, makes the point that every relationship has a high-desire partner and a low-desire partner. He assures us that this is normal. Sometimes the high-desire partner is the woman; often it is the man. The high-desire partner may feel that the low-desire partner isn't loving enough or giving enough. The low-desire partner may wonder why everything comes down to sex. Couples become frustrated with each other. They begin to question themselves: "What's wrong with us? What's wrong with our relationship?"

"We're too pooped to whoop!"

Clearly, this difference in levels of desire will require compromise and sacrifice on both sides; it will require *agape*, sacrificial love that in this case seeks to bless the other by making love more often, or less often, than each might desire. Sacrificial love is one part of the dance we learn in order to have a terrific intimate life, bonding and deepening our love for one another as God intended.

Another part of the dance is creativity: How do you keep from becoming bored? If you are with the same person for thirty to forty years and do the same thing every time, you'll certainly be bored. So it's important to be intentionally creative, making your intimate life playful and exciting. Be careful, though, not to have unrealistic expectations. If we liken sexual intimacy to a meal, not every dinner will be a five-course gourmet event. It takes hours of thought and preparation to enjoy a five-course meal, and usually we don't have the time or energy. But we may have time for pizza, fast food, or a peanut butter and jelly sandwich.

How Often and What It Means

Just as it's important not to be unrealistic about the quality of our intimate experiences, we shouldn't be unrealistic about the quantity of these experiences. Most guys I talk to want more intimacy. They assume that everyone else is having a lot more sex than they are. Then they have a little pity party because they feel that they are missing out.

With this issue in mind, we asked the people who took our survey how frequently they were intimate with their mates. Let's take a look at the results and what we learn from them.

Frequency of Sexual Intimacy

Age	3x/week	2x/week	1x/week	2x/month	1x/month	Less/never
19–29	11%	22%	35%	21%	6%	5%
30–39	6%	15%	26%	29%	10%	14%
40–49	6%	14%	26%	22%	12%	19%
50–59	4%	8%	28%	17%	11%	32%
60–69	2%	7%	24%	16%	11%	40%
70–79	3%	2%	10%	20%	10%	53%
80–89	0%	0%	7%	4%	11%	78%

Only 11 percent of couples in their 20s made love three times a week or more. When I got married, I thought most guys were making love three or four nights a week, but in reality very few couples, even in their 20s, make love that often. Among those in their 20s, 22 percent made love twice a week, 35 percent once a week, 21 percent twice a month, and about 10 percent less frequently than that.

From the comments there was one word that explained it more than any other: *children*.

Let's look at what happens when we move to the 30s. Among our respondents, intimacy dropped dramatically, and from the comments there was one word that explained it more than any other: *children*. The category "three times a week" dropped by nearly half, "two times a week" by a third, and "one time a week" by a fourth. In fact, nearly 80 percent of respondents in their 30s made love once a week or less, and the largest group made love twice a month.

In the 40s, the high end stabilizes: about 45 percent of people in their 40s made love at least once a week. But now just over 50 percent made love less than once a week. Based on the comments and my own experience in counseling, the greatest marital dissatisfaction occurs when people are in their 40s.

In the 50s, the number of people who made love more than once a week and the number who made love less than once a week are roughly equal. Health-related problems became bigger issues—for women, menopause; for men, prostate and erectile dysfunction. Surprisingly, though, while frequency dropped, the comments from both men and women indicated that satisfaction increased.

In the 60s, 33 percent of respondents made love once a week or more, and of those, most indicated once a week. This reflected a continued gradual decrease in sexual frequency, but once again, comments indicated that satisfaction increased.

In the 70s, the number of respondents making love once a week or more drops by half, to 15 percent, with a handful of very energetic 70-somethings still making love three times a week. (You're giving the rest of us hope!) The survey showed that 70 percent of couples were still sexually active in their 70s, though for many that meant less than once a month. And guess what—the comments indicated that for couples in their 70s, sexual satisfaction reached a new high.

We had a much smaller group of respondents in their 80s, 37 percent of whom were still sexually active while 63 percent were not. Yet once again, people in their 80s reported greater satisfaction with their intimate lives than people in their 20s, 30s, 40s, 50s, or 60s. So, while frequency declines with age, satisfaction and happiness with this part of our lives seems to increase.

Our findings suggested a correlation between marital happiness and frequency of sexual intimacy. It's hard to know which leads to which: Does frequent sexual intimacy lead to greater happiness and fulfillment in marriage, or do greater happiness and fulfillment in marriage lead to frequent sexual intimacy? The answer probably is a bit of both. We did find in our survey that 56 percent of those who indicated they were "very unhappy" in their marriage never made love. And 55 percent of those who were "very happy" made love at least once a week. We also noted that 72 percent of those who made love three times a week or more reported being "very happy."

Hints and Suggestions

Given that most couples experience a degree of frustration over intimacy at some point in their marriage, I'd like to offer a few suggestions. These come from listening to couples who improved the quality of their intimate life and from reading books by sex therapists who described strategies found to be helpful. Some of the suggestions may seem odd coming from a pastor or a book by a Christian author. You might giggle at some or think they sound ridiculous, but if you are not completely satisfied with your intimate relationship, you might want to consider them.

1. Schedule days for making love.

Scheduled lovemaking, as unromantic as that might sound, has been very helpful to many couples. One of our respondents said that for years she and her husband had argued about frequency of intimacy, until they agreed to make love two days a week, Mondays and Fridays. It was less than the three days he would have preferred and more than the one day she would have preferred. Knowing they would make love on those two days removed the guesswork, which had been a source of frustration for both of them.

She indicated that in the past, he was always wondering, *Could this be the night?* And whenever he gave her a hug or kiss, she would always wonder, *Does he really want to bless me, or is he hoping for more?* But when they agreed on Mondays and Fridays, both of them were ready, at some point in the day, to share in intimate touch and lovemaking.

Every back rub, every foot rub, every cuddle comes with no strings attached.

This could be something to plan your day around. It doesn't matter how tired you are (unless you agree to swap nights, which is easy enough) — you can initiate one time, your partner the next. On the other nights of the week, every back rub, every foot rub, every cuddle comes with no strings attached.

Scheduled lovemaking may not work for everyone, but it is one strategy to address the guesswork and frustration that often accompany lovemaking.

2. See lovemaking as part of the mission of marriage.

If we see marriage as a mission and sacred calling to bless our mate, then lovemaking and non-sexual touch will be important ways of fulfilling this calling. When two people are committed to seeking ways to bless each other, sexual intimacy can only improve. When the lower-desire partner sees sexual intimacy as a way to minister to and bless his or her partner, the act of making love becomes an act of self-giving, a way of making a deposit in the partner's love bank. Likewise, if you are the higher-desire partner, then offering hand rubs, foot rubs, hand holding, and cuddling for their own sake and not as a prelude to sex can be seen as a way to bless your mate.

3. Make intimate times fun and playful.

Lovemaking is meant to be pleasurable, enjoyable, and fun—yes, fun. But often, over the years, lovemaking becomes routine, predictable, and boring. In the survey's open-ended comments, many people described their lovemaking as boring.

Lovemaking is a chance, as grownups, to rediscover play.

And just as some think everyone is having more sex than they are, many couples believe everyone is having more interesting sex than they are. Most people who have been married for more than a few years find it easy to get into a rut when it comes to making love. The good news is that, with an investment of time, emotional energy, and creativity, this part of your life can be improved, and spice can be added to a bland intimate relationship.

You'll find a list of suggestions below, based on advice I've read from experts or heard from couples in counseling. (Note that I'm intentionally not sharing things from my personal life here. One of the key elements of trust is that your partner must know you will not tell others such information, and sharing details about my own intimate life would violate that trust.)

- Bad hygiene is a turnoff, so brush your teeth, take a shower, use cologne or perfume, and dress in a way that will appeal to your mate. If you are going out on a date, look your best.

- If you have agreed to make love on a certain night, try your best to do loving things toward your mate throughout the day, such as a note, text, or e-mail expressing your love, or a hug, kiss, or touch that communicates love and romance.

- Think in advance about your lovemaking. Be creative about where and how you'll make love. There are some good books to help you do this, but one thing I'd suggest is to think of lovemaking, at least sometimes, as play with your best friend. When you were children you made up games and role-played with your friends. Lovemaking is a chance, as grownups, to rediscover play.

- With increasing frequency we're seeing television ads for "toys" meant to enhance the experience of intimacy. While I'm not a fan of having these commercials play on television, the use of such toys has helped many people improve the quality of their intimate life. Sex therapists note that this is particularly true for women, who find that these can increase the likelihood of climax, and can increase the playfulness and excitement for both partners.

- A back rub, foot rub, or hand rub can do wonders to relax a mate who may not be in the mood, and sometimes this act of self-giving will open the door to more intimate touch. There should also be times, though, when these acts are done without leading to sexual intimacy.

- Sexy lingerie is a blessing to couples who are feeling their love life is stuck in a rut, for both the wife and her husband. Candles can set the mood for both sexes. Romantic music adds to the ambiance.

- If you have small children, one of the most important things you can do is to schedule a half dozen times a year when the children stay with grandparents or friends and you plan a romantic getaway. It can be in your own home or at a hotel with a romantic dinner. Many couples with small children feel guilty about leaving their kids, but if these times away deepen your love for each other and help you reconnect, they will make you better parents when you come back.

- Finally, you may find it helpful to read one of the many books written by sex therapists aimed at helping couples rekindle the flame. Read the book together, discuss it, and try out some of the suggestions.

Most of you already know these things. What I've found, though, is that couples sometimes lack the energy even to try them. Your intimate relationship is not meant to be dull or boring. It is a gift from God that can bind you together. But remember, not every time you make love will be a gourmet experience. Most people eat far more PB&J sandwiches than gourmet meals!

A Few Final Tips

The survey results and comments included some interesting tips and correlations. We wanted to know more about the people, aged 20–59, who were involved with each other intimately at least twice a week.

It turned out that 71 percent of these people made it a point to go on a date at least monthly, as compared with an average of less than once a month for survey respondents overall. Of course, once again the chicken-and-egg question comes to mind: Are couples who date regularly more likely to be intimate with each other, or does getting intimate make them want to go out more? Whichever it is, or whether it's a little of both, clearly there's a correlation.

Our survey showed a definite correlation between physical intimacy and spiritual intimacy!

We also discovered that 57 percent of the people who were intimate twice a week spent at least 30 minutes a day in conversation, against an overall average of 15 minutes. These folks had learned that physical intimacy leads to quality talk, or perhaps that quality talk leads to greater intimacy. Again, our survey showed a real connection between the two.

Of the people who were intimate twice a week, fully 80 percent attended worship regularly! That's an interesting statistic. If you look at the responses of people who seldom or never attended worship, they were just one-third as likely to be physically intimate twice a week. What's more, it turned out that people who prayed together daily were twice as likely to make love two times a week as those who seldom or never prayed together. By both these measures, our survey showed a definite correlation between physical intimacy and spiritual intimacy!

This mingling of the physical and spiritual is very much in keeping with what Paul wrote in the Scripture that opens this chapter. The passage is a remarkable one. It says the wife's body belongs to the husband, and the husband's to the wife. Paul's words become even more striking when put in context. He was writing to the church at Corinth, which you might call the French Quarter of the first century. Corinth was a port city that teemed with sailors looking for diversion, and it was said that a thousand temple prostitutes helped provide it. Sexual immorality was rampant. And yet, in this city people were coming to Christ. Some of those who were married wrote to Paul, saying in essence, "We know that the kind of sex all around us is bad. Does that mean we shouldn't have sex unless we want a baby?"

In paraphrase, Paul answered, "Heavens, no! You're supposed to be intimate with each other! It's a blessing from God. And here's what you need to know: Husbands, your body isn't yours; it belongs to your wife. What does she need? A tender touch? A listening ear? Use your body to bless her! Wives, your body belongs to your husband. How can you bless him? What can you do to minister to him, encourage him, lift him up, and fill him with joy?"

In this passage, Paul made it clear that sexual intimacy can be an expression of *agape*, our desire to love selflessly. In this, it embodies the very idea of marriage: two people bound together, naked before one another, giving themselves to each other. It takes work, intentionality, and sacrifice, but when we get it right it plays a crucial role in making love last a lifetime. As both partners minister to one another, they find through the blessing of sexual intimacy the riches God intended for them.

One of our respondents, a woman in her 70s, wrote a note on the survey. The note said health problems made it impossible for the woman and her husband to have intimate relations anymore, but that they had discovered many ways to express physical love. She mentioned hugs and kisses, loving looks, and touches. "And we flirt with each other all the time," she said. "People feel deeply in love without physical sex prior to marriage, and while sex is a joyous part of marriage, it is not the only measure of deep love and sharing."

That woman's wise words may be the most important thing to take away from this chapter — that in the end, love and intimacy involve much more than just sex. Interestingly, our survey showed that those most satisfied with the physical aspect of their marriages were older adults who, though having intercourse far less frequently than others, often for health reasons, found that physical touch continued to be hugely important in their lives.

REFLECT AND ENGAGE

Scheduled Intimacy

It's no secret that the novelty of sex wears off when you've been together a while. Eventually, jobs and long commutes, preparing and cleaning up from dinner, and the arrival of kids make it more and more tempting to hit the sack with little more than a kiss goodnight or a drowsy pat over the covers. While every marriage is different, the day will likely come when you have sex less because you're "in the mood" and more because "we should." The nice thing, though, is that even "we should" sex is enjoyable and brings you closer, even if you weren't in the mood at the start.

It's important to remember that sexual intimacy involves so much more than the act of intercourse itself, and a lot of the kisses and touches that were so exciting earlier in your relationship can fall by the wayside even more easily than intercourse. Especially if one partner enjoys these things more than intercourse, he or she may feel frustrated and shortchanged by your sex life.

Whether or not you are satisfied with your current frequency of sex (and chances are rare that both spouses are equally satisfied), this experiment can be enlightening as you seek to know one another better—in the biblical sense.

Choose two evenings in the next week when you will have time to spend together. Designate one night when you will definitely have sex—in the mood or not, tired or not—and then schedule another night when you will be intimate together without having intercourse. Later in the week, discuss the following questions.

• Which evening did each of you enjoy more? Why? If you disagree about which was more enjoyable, what can you do about that?

• What did it feel like to be expecting sex on the day it was "scheduled"? How did you feel once the time grew closer, and once you having intercourse?

• On the day when you scheduled intimacy but not intercourse, what did it feel like to know you would only be going "so far"? Did you rediscover anything you forgot you enjoyed, or feel frustrated by restraining yourselves? Did you end up having sex anyway?

• Knowing that compromise is necessary, what plans can you make for your sex life going forward that would be appealing to both of you and draw you closer in your intimacy as a couple?

Pray Together

Dear God, thank you for the gift of sex and the joys of our physical bodies. We are sorry for when we trivialize this gift or selfishly make it about our own gratification. Help us to serve one another in the bedroom as we would anywhere else, and to see sex as a valuable part of our love and commitment to one another. Amen.

On Your Own

How do you feel about the points at which you and your partner differ on sex? Knowing the importance of putting the other's needs before your own, what are some ways you can sacrifice or expand your own preferences in order to bless your partner?

If You're Single

You see sex all around you, from commercials on TV, to magazine articles, to the giant posters in front of Victoria's Secret. With such an emphasis on sex and sexiness, it can be easy to start thinking of your body in those terms and judging your body by the standards you see in media. But your body is for much more than sex. What other ways can your body express who you are?

4

HABITS THAT HURT, HABITS THAT HEAL

Let no evil talk come out of your mouths, but only what is useful for building up, as there is need, so that your words may give grace to those who hear.

Ephesians 4:29

For this is the will of God, your sanctification: that you abstain from [sexual immorality]; that each one of you know how to control your own body in holiness and honor.

1 Thessalonians 4:3-4

Let your fountain be blessed,
*   and rejoice in the wife of your youth,*
*   a lovely deer, a graceful doe…*
*   may you be intoxicated always by her love.*
Why should you be intoxicated, my son, by another woman?

Proverbs 5:18-20a

One of my church members recently sent me a photo of an older couple sitting on a park bench. In a caption the husband says, "Whenever I get mad you never seem to get upset. How do you manage to control your temper?"

She replies, "I just go and clean the toilet."

"How does that help?" he asks.

"I use your toothbrush," she answers.

Even the most loving couples in the most satisfying relationships are going to have conflicts. Most are small, involving the petty irritants that lead to bickering and low-level disagreements. Healthy couples work through these things or laugh them off, so the little conflicts don't escalate into something more.

When we enter into a persistent pattern of speaking with contempt toward our mate, we are undercutting the supports of the partnership that is marriage.

But occasionally there are really big issues, the kind that can shipwreck a relationship. These transgressions bring nothing but pain. We asked the 1,305 divorced persons who took our Love, Sex, and Marriage survey to help us understand the big conflicts that helped to destroy their marriages. In this chapter I'll share with you some of what we learned, and we'll discuss how to avoid habits that hurt and practice habits that heal.

In the survey responses, divorced persons identified a host of causes that led to the failure of their marriages—poor communication, money problems, marrying too young, turning away from each other—but in this chapter we will focus on the top three issues they cited. It would be hard to overstate the damage caused by each of these or how seriously we need to take them.

I challenge you, therefore, to join me in considering these threats and learning how to address them or to avoid them. The three issues, in order of frequency mentioned in the surveys, are adultery, addiction, and emotional or physical abuse. We will look at them in reverse order.

Emotional or Physical Abuse

Every fifteen seconds in the United States, a woman is battered by her husband or boyfriend. Every day, four of these women will die.[11] There are instances in which women perpetrate violence, but by and large it is men.

Abuse takes many forms. One is verbal abuse, a form of emotional violence that leaves psychological scars. Often the men who undertake this kind of behavior are charming and personable. They may be very successful in their careers. Sometimes no one but the spouse or girlfriend sees the switch thrown when they get home, sees them demean and belittle their partners, making them feel small and worthless.

When we enter into a persistent pattern of speaking with contempt toward our mate, we are undercutting the supports of the partnership that is marriage.

I have also seen remarkable, seemingly godly women who lead Bible studies and do all sorts of charitable work treat their husbands miserably, demeaning them and making them feel small at home or in front of others.

All of us say things we should not say, but when we enter into a persistent pattern of demeaning, of speaking with contempt toward our mate, we are undercutting the supports of the partnership that is marriage.

John Gottman, professor emeritus of psychology at the University of Washington and a leading authority on marriage, says that people in great marriages fight now and then, some of them every day. But, he says, it's not how often couples fight but how they fight that determines whether a marriage is great. He has famously claimed that within the first five minutes of meeting with a couple, he can discern with 91 percent accuracy whether they will ultimately divorce. He does so by setting up a question that's bound to cause conflict, then watching to see how they fight. Do they express frustration about the situation, or do they go on the attack, demeaning and abusing each other? That latter response, he says, is a sign of impending shipwreck.[12]

Sometimes abuse takes the form of intimidation, of withholding love, or of exercising control over the other. Some seek to control the finances or the partner's schedule, directing every behavior until finally the spouse no longer feels any autonomy.

Sometimes, of course, there is physical violence. Crossing that line means taking a serious step toward destroying the marriage.

We have seen that marriage is a calling from God, a covenant in which we are commissioned by God to bless, minister to, build up, and seek the best for each other. We are called to be helpers and companions, allowing our partners to flourish and experience God's riches. Harming our mates, physically or emotionally, or controlling and demeaning them, is the exact opposite of this vow.

Paul, while recognizing the tendency we sometimes have to belittle others or hurt them by our words and actions, describes the Christian ideal in Ephesians 4:

> Let no evil talk come out of your mouths, but only what is useful for building up as there is need, so that your words may give grace to those who hear. And do not grieve the Holy Spirit of God with which you are marked with a seal for the day of redemption. Put away from you all bitterness and wrath and anger and wrangling and slander, together with all malice, and be kind to one another, tenderhearted, forgiving one another as God in Christ has forgiven you. (vv. 29-32)

The Greek word for evil, used here in the phrase "evil talk," means to putrefy. It signifies something that is rotting, the kind of thing you find in the forgotten Tupperware at the back of the refrigerator. You open it and the smell staggers you. That is the image Paul uses for the kind of words we speak that bring pain to others, words that he tells us Christians are not to use.

Jesus himself says something similar. When the Pharisees upbraid Jesus because his disciples are eating before they wash their hands, making them ceremonially unclean, Jesus says, "Listen, it's not what you put in your mouth that makes you unclean. It is what comes out of your mouth, because that comes from the heart" (Matthew 15:17-18, paraphrase). Spewing vile words at someone — especially our mate — is an indication of the sickness sometimes resident within us.

When it comes to physical and emotional abuse in marriage, the Christian church hasn't always helped the situation. In that same letter to the Ephesians, Paul writes that women are to submit to their husbands. Paul lived in a patriarchal society in which women were considered to be the property of their fathers or husbands. His epistle actually elevated the status of women relative to the broader society, but the church sometimes has interpreted this particular passage to mean that the man is the boss, the overlord of the woman, and that he can do with her what he likes. We forget Paul has just said that evil words should not come out of our mouths. We forget he has said we are to submit mutually to each other, that husbands are to love their wives as Christ loved the church and gave himself up for her.

I don't believe God intended marriage to be a prison sentence.

Pastors often turn to the Scriptures to emphasize the fact that God hates divorce—and he does—but too often we use that as a chain to bind the woman or man in an abusive, soul-killing marriage. I have known people who were in abusive relationships and whose families encouraged them to remain in the marriage because "God hates divorce." Yes, God hates divorce, but I think there are some things God hates even more. Watching his children being abused physically or emotionally by their mates is one of them.

I don't believe God intended marriage to be a prison sentence in which one partner suffers emotional and physical abuse for the rest of his or her life. In such cases the abusive mate has already torn apart the marriage covenant. The challenge is to discern what constitutes abuse. If you are physically being harmed by your mate, it is abuse. It is never God's intention that a woman or man be trapped in a physically abusive relationship. But what about abuse that is not physical? Here it may be helpful to talk with a counselor to gain help in understanding when a persistent behavior rises to the level of abuse and is unlikely to be resolved.

As a spouse, you are meant to help, bless, build, lift up, and encourage. Are you doing those things? Or are you persistently criticizing, belittling, and tearing down? The former is what a healthy relationship is mean to be like. The latter can easily be classified as abuse.

If you are being abused, there is help. There are agencies and counselors, shelters and ministries designed to support you. If you are an abuser, there is help to get out of that as well. But in either case, you've got to have the courage to say, "I know this is not right. Something's got to change. I need help." You've got to be willing to seek the aid of God and other people.

Addiction

Classically, the addiction that ruined marriages — and so much more — was alcohol abuse. In the last fifty years, though, we have seen the increase of drug abuse and gambling. More recently sexual addiction, particularly as it relates to Internet pornography, has become part of the picture.

Addiction begins with the promise of pleasure. Unfortunately, after the initial pleasure — often occurring when certain biochemicals are released in the brain—we quickly want another shot of these chemicals. We pursue the same activity again, receiving another biochemical jolt, but this time the satisfaction doesn't last as long, and we find ourselves craving another shot of pleasure. After a while, what first was enjoyable is no longer enough, and we need more stimuli to get the same response. Over time the behavior becomes self-destructive, and we become enslaved to what was once pleasurable.

If your wife or husband says, "I think you have a drinking problem," you probably do.

Of course, not everyone reacts that way. Some people can walk into a casino, spend twenty bucks, and leave. Others spend the same twenty dollars and can't stop. Twenty dollars becomes fifty and then five hundred. Pretty soon, they're looking for ways to take money out of retirement accounts to feed a compulsion they can't overcome. Individuals and families are brought to ruin every day by addiction to drugs, gambling, sex, and alcohol.

Addictions affect the lives of everyone in the house, and they ripple through ensuing generations. Often those closest to the person involved are the first to see the addiction. If your wife or husband says, "I think you have a drinking problem," you probably do. The good news is that you can be set free, but you have to face the situation and ask yourself, "Is my desire to drink (or whatever your addiction may be) worth destroying or hurting the people I love most?" Know that there is plenty of help available. For some, simply joining a Celebrate Recovery or Alcoholics Anonymous group and working the program will be enough. Others will need inpatient or outpatient treatment. Millions of people have defeated their addictions and, with the help of God, you can too.

People struggle with addictions of many kinds, but in this section I'll focus on a form of addiction that in recent years has reached epidemic proportions in our society. Let's discuss sexual addiction and Internet pornography. This powerful addiction affects average people and, as the headlines tell us, also affects some of the most powerful leaders in the country. That's just one part of the problem. Another part is the devastating effect Internet pornography can have on children. When I was a child, I remember sneaking peaks at the naked women in my dad's copies of Playboy. That was a fairly common introduction to sex for many boys in generations past. But now, any savvy fourth grader can access pornography on the Internet, working around parental controls if their parents even bother to use them, and see sexual expressions no child should see. Those images help form the child's ideas about the roles of men and women, how they relate, what sexual intimacy is, and how it works. And those images can be as addictive to children as they are to adults.

As we've discussed, sexual intimacy releases certain chemicals in the brain that link us to the person with whom we share intimacy. They are designed to reinforce our partnership with a mate: we feel pleasure, and we're drawn back to them. Those chemicals are the super-glue that holds relationships together. But those same chemicals are released when we view pornography and stimulate ourselves, and the bonding that is meant to draw us to our mate actually leads us to need and want more stimulation — in other words, we bond with pornography and self-stimulation. Then the desire to repeat that chemical high draws us back to those images again and again.

I read an article not long ago by a woman who was a porn star in the 1990s. She talked about the way some women are pushed into the industry by their boyfriends or pimps, while others are desperate for the money. The movies often portray women on the receiving end of violence as though they are enjoying the experience. She described being on the sets of these films and watching women go into the bathroom between scenes to vomit before returning to the set.[13] These are the kinds of things we don't see on the screen.

Viewing pornography triggers physiological reactions that make us want to see more. Men are visual by nature. Our desire to see these things doesn't make us terrible people; it just means we're human. But it's a short journey to a place where the desire for more stimulation cascades out of control. The pornography you started with no longer excites you. You become desensitized. You want something more to get the same level of excitement you once felt. So the pornography becomes harder and more depraved. Eventually you may reach the point where it isn't enough to see it; you want to experience it yourself. The risks become greater — to your health, your finances, your reputation, your family. You become a slave. And though in the past it was mostly men who fell into this trap, today an increasing number of women are struggling with pornography.

A fellow preacher at a nearby church shared with me his own story of addiction to pornography. Here is part of his story in his own words:

When I stumbled into Internet pornography, keep in mind at this point in life I'm a professional Christian. I'm a pastor. I really believe the gospel I'm preaching. And I hated myself. I promised God. I'd say, "I will not do this again. I know this is wrong. I know you don't want me living this way. And I want to be the kind of person that you're pleased with." And I meant it. I honestly said, "That's it. I'm done. I've turned the corner." Till the next time, when the shame was even greater.

The life of an addict or a compulsive person is a life of dichotomy. On the one hand I'm married to my wife Pam. I love Pam. I care deeply about Pam. I don't want to hurt her. On the other hand I'm living in secrets. And once I finally told her, it was crushing to her. I had ruined everything. I had now destroyed my ministry, my church, my marriage, my family. I didn't have any hope. But I still had faith. And it was that faith that brought me through to a place where hope began to come into my soul again.

Have I arrived at where I need to be? No. Have I arrived at where I want to be? No. I'm on a journey. It took therapy. It took people. It took breaking down all kinds of barriers. And it took me blowing up my life until I got to that place where eventually I finally got free.[14]

It has now been several years since T.C. Ryan, the preacher who wrote those words, overcame his sexual addiction. He describes the experience in his book *Ashamed No More*. The book may be very helpful for some of you reading this chapter.

We asked the married people in our Love, Sex and Marriage survey about their viewing of pornography. Just eight percent of women under 60 reported viewing pornography occasionally — although we didn't ask precisely what "occasionally" meant — and only a very few said "frequently." When it came to men, though, pornography seemed to be a much bigger issue. Here's what we found:

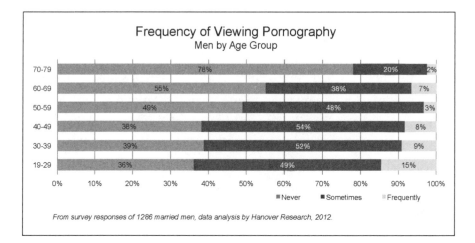

From survey responses of 1286 married men, data analysis by Hanover Research, 2012.

Nearly two-thirds of the guys from their 20s through their 40s viewed pornography, a figure that dropped to about half in their 50s and 60s and to about one fifth in their 70s. Keep in mind that these are married men, most of whom would call themselves Christians and many of whom worship regularly in the church I serve. That tells me this is a big issue.

That's not to say that everyone who views pornography once in a while is addicted to it. The results of our survey suggest that most younger men view pornography sometimes. I'm also not suggesting that there is an immediate and dire physical or psychological price to pay for using it. But for many, what starts out as self-gratification can lead to pain. It takes more self-discipline than many possess to say, "No more." For some, pornography is a gateway experience leading to addiction, risky and inappropriate sexual behavior, adultery, and other behaviors that can have devastating consequences.

First-century Christians were not immune to this struggle. Many of them lived in a highly sexualized society, and Paul and the other apostles spoke about the challenges of what we would call sexual addiction. The Greek word Paul used for sexual immorality, for acting in ways that make you a slave to sex, was *porneio,* from which we derive our word pornography.

In 1 Thessalonians 4:3-5*a*, Paul writes, "For this is the will of God, your sanctification, that you abstain from sexual immorality, that each one of you know how to control your own body in holiness and honor, not with lustful passion."

**We are to choose those paths that lead
to holiness of heart and mind,
paths that lead to wholeness and life.**

Elsewhere Paul says all things are permissible but not all things are beneficial. There are some things we should choose not to do, not because doing it once or twice will destroy us, but because we know the behavior can lead to addiction, pain, or shame, and so ideally we choose to say, "I'm not going to do it." That is how Paul encourages us to respond. We are to reject those paths in life that enslave us, hurt others, or dishonor God, and, by practicing self-discipline and restraint, we are to choose those paths that lead to holiness of heart and mind, paths that lead to wholeness and life.

The pervasiveness of pornography and its ready availability on the Internet makes sexual addiction even more challenging for many today. However, it is not impossible to resist this ubiquitous temptation, and even those who are addicted can find liberation. With God's power and a network of supportive people around us, we can be freed, because God doesn't want us to be enslaved by anything. Marriages can be healed of the pain that comes from these addictions.

Sexual addiction is not a death sentence for a marriage, but the issues must be addressed. We can find freedom and healing by turning to God, being honest with those we love, being aware of the potential dangers, and accepting the grace of God. Healing usually includes disciplines aimed at resting temptation. Celebrate Recovery and Sexaholics Anonymous are two organized fellowships that help people practice such disciplines and find freedom. Visiting with a pastor or counselor with experience dealing with sexual addiction can also be immensely helpful.

Adultery

The most prevalent danger to marriages and the leading cause of divorce is adultery, and that is true across cultures. In

150 countries around the world, the number-one cause of divorce is infidelity.[15]

Of course, often infidelity is a symptom of a much deeper problem. Sometimes, however, it is the primary problem. In either case, it is the leading cause of shipwreck in marriage. In our own survey, both men and women ranked this at the top.

We should begin by stating that attraction to someone else is not the problem. In fact, without even meaning to, most of us have our antennae up pretty much all the time. We are wired to recognize attractive people as potential mates. That doesn't end when we marry, just as it doesn't begin when we marry. Back in junior high, we were eyeing those of the opposite sex, wondering whether or not they might like us. Such attraction is a normal part of being human.

Sometimes we run across people with whom we feel real chemistry. Sometimes it's momentary excitement and sexual tension, and sometimes it's a deeper emotional connection. If we weren't susceptible to that sort of attraction—and if the consequences of acting on it weren't so potentially devastating— then "Thou shalt not commit adultery" wouldn't have made the Top Ten list among the 613 commandments found in the Hebrew Scripture. It's the reason our marriage vows include the question, "Will you forsake all others and be faithful to him (or her) alone as long as you both shall live?" Because we can be tempted, the wedding vow makes it clear that we will shut off every other option, which is a tall but necessary order. We are saying, "For the rest of my life I will give myself and my heart to no one but you." That is what we promise when we take the wedding vow. But that vow doesn't mean we won't ever feel drawn to someone who is not our mate.

I once visited a friend who was watching a country music award show on TV, and a video of Faith Hill's song "Breathe" was playing. I'd never seen Faith Hill before, but there she was on his TV screen. She is an amazingly beautiful woman. My heart beat faster. I thought, *My gosh, she's the one. This is the woman I was supposed to marry. And her name is Faith! It's a sure sign from God.* (Hear my exaggerated humor here!)

My little fantasy ended at that point, but it was a vivid example of how stupid our thinking can be when we're attracted to people we don't happen to be married to. We're human beings, and those feelings can rise up. The question in a case like that is the same question we face when confronted with pornography: *What do I do with this? How do I deal with the excitement?* As with other human emotions, including anger, the feeling serves a purpose in its proper place, but it can easily take us off in another direction that leads only to pain.

In designing our survey we wanted an idea of how many people had struggled with infidelity, so we asked respondents whether they had ever been unfaithful. Of the 3,856 married people who took part—and remember, these were members of our church or were otherwise affiliated with it—just 11 percent of married men and 6 percent of married women had been unfaithful. Let's compare these figures with national averages reported by Dr. W. Bradford Wilcox, Director of the National Marriage Project at the University of Virginia. He reports that 22 percent of men who've ever been married, and 14 percent of women who've ever married, have had an extra-marital affair in their lifetime.[16]

Looking at these numbers, I wondered if they were evidence that religious involvement is related to a lower incidence of infidelity. I'll confess that I wanted reassurance because I was a little skeptical of our numbers. I was hopeful that the members of our congregation were not exaggerating their faithfulness to their spouses.

I was interested and relieved to see that the University of Chicago's General Social Survey did in fact show that regular attendance at worship has a significant impact on marital fidelity. It looks like this: Of those who never attend services, the rate of reported adultery is 24.8 percent. For those who attend less than monthly, the rate is 20.6 percent. For those attending monthly or more it is 17.1 percent, and for those attending weekly it is 12.4 percent.[17]

If we want to affair-proof our marriage, attending worship together is a great place to start.

Results of the General Social Survey don't include speculation about the connection between worship and fidelity, but I'd like to offer a thought or two about why worship seems to cause a lower occurrence of infidelity. Weekly worship reminds us of who we are as God's children and of our desire to do God's will. It reminds us of our core values and ideals. Worshiping in a community links us with others who share our values, encourage us, and exert a kind of positive peer pressure toward doing what we believe is right.

But I think there is more. As we worship, pray, share the Eucharist, and listen for God to speak, we are spiritually fed and thereby given strength to resist the temptations that we face. We connect with God and find the power of the Holy Spirit working in us to empower, guide, and shape us. This same Spirit convicts us when we find ourselves on that slippery slope between, say, attraction and infidelity. So, if we want to affair-proof our marriage, attending worship together is a great place to start. It's not a guarantee, but it appears to cut the risk in half.

In addition to worship, there are practical aids to strengthening marriages and fighting infidelity. One is simply understanding how infidelity happens. Dozens of people have come into my office through the years to confess that they have been unfaithful. The stories I hear fall generally into two categories. The first is people who are traveling and participate in "one-night stands." In a moment of weakness they succumb to desire, and afterward they feel terrible guilt and desperately want to make things right.

The other category is people who develop emotional bonds with someone over a long period of time. It used to be that the number-one place this happened was the workplace. The day-in, day-out presence of someone with whom you're working toward common goals, sometimes on a particular project, can be exciting. Then you go home to dinner and chores and a spouse who's had a rough day. You try to talk with your spouse about the exciting things happening at work, but the spouse isn't nearly as excited about them as you are.

You go back to work the next day and see your co-worker, who is dressed for work, who isn't asking you to take out the trash, who is excited to talk about your job and your shared projects. You might spend more time interacting with this person than with your mate. You go home again at the end of the day to find a tired spouse, household frustrations, needy kids, bills that are due, and, once again, very little interest in the work that excites you.

This is the time when red flags should be out, the time to watch for what Lutheran pastor and author Walter Wangerin called "the moment of maybe."[18] It's the moment when you begin to think, *God forbid anything should happen to my husband (or wife), but if it did, I could picture myself with this other man (or woman).* Or it may be simply an idle, *I wonder what it would be like to be with her (or him)?*

You find yourself thinking about it more, and one day you finally say something like, "I wish my husband were more like you" or "If only my wife were as understanding as you are" or, worse, "I find you so attractive." What happens then? Nothing good, to be sure. Either the person does not feel the same way and now is uncomfortable around you, or the person does feel the same way and you've opened the door to an affair.

At some point there's that "accidental" touch and the friendly hug that lasts just a little too long. You can't stop thinking about the other person, all the while telling yourself you'd never let anything happen. And then comes the moment when you step across a line that makes the affair nearly inevitable.

The New Testament epistle of James says it this way: "One is tempted by one's own desire, being lured and enticed by it; then when that desire has conceived, it gives birth to sin, and that sin, when it is fully grown, gives birth to death" (James 1:14-15).

In a case such as this, it is vital to set up boundaries, recognize the warning signs, and back off before the attraction goes too far.

This kind of situation used to arise mainly in the workplace, but today the primary conduit for potential marital problems is Facebook and other social media. That's the conclusion of some studies done with divorce attorneys: today Facebook is where most of these connections are made.[19] You run across an old high-school or college flame. A false intimacy develops in the privacy of an online conversation. It's fun and exciting. At that point you can even tell your spouse, "Guess who I ran into on Facebook!"

Over time you reveal more personal and intimate details. You share your deepest thoughts and feelings, and the person responds in kind. If your spouse walks into the room during one of these online conversations, you quickly close the window because you don't want her to see what you're saying. That, of course, should raise huge warning flags.

You begin texting back and forth. You flirt. And then one day, you go on a trip to the person's city. "What if we meet up?" you say. That is how many affairs begin today.

Boundaries and Strategies

How do you set up boundaries to keep you from infidelity? How do you build firewalls to keep the early conversations from turning into full-fledged emotional and then physical affairs?

The spark is a warning signal, and in a healthy relationship you set up guardrails to protect your heart and marriage.

LaVon and I have been married for thirty years, and there have been several times when I've felt that momentary spark of excitement toward someone else. As we've said, there is nothing wrong with the spark itself; it just means you're human. The challenge is what you do about it. The spark is a warning signal, and in a healthy relationship you set up guardrails to protect your heart and marriage. Here are some ways LaVon and I have tried to protect ours.

On rare occasions in the past twenty-five years, a woman has come to me and said, "I want you to know that I'm attracted to you." I'm a somewhat balding middle-aged guy, but I have learned over the years that the office of pastor makes otherwise unattractive pastors seem attractive. When it happens to me, the first person I tell is LaVon. This diffuses the power of the secret, and it enlists her as a partner in addressing the issue.

I also give LaVon all my passwords—Facebook, e-mail, everything. There's nothing she can't read. She has access to every thought I've ever had that made it onto my computer screen. That protects me as well as her. It fosters trust and makes me accountable for the ways I communicate with others. Though she never looks at my communications, I want her to know, and I want to know, that she could look at any time.

I recall hearing that Billy Graham once was invited to a private meeting with Hillary Clinton, whose husband Bill Clinton was at that time the governor of Arkansas. Graham indicated he would be pleased to meet with her but only in a public place, as he had a rule against being alone with a woman who was not his wife. The press found it humorous, but Graham was unapologetic. It was a rule he had put in place many years earlier to protect himself, and he had never set it aside.[20]

You are a child of God, a husband or wife, a parent, a friend. Is the behavior you are considering consistent with these roles?

Think through the consequences of succumbing to temptation—I can't stress too strongly the importance of doing so. Often people succumb to temptation because they haven't thought about the likely outcome.

A man in my congregation described the day his wife discovered he'd had an affair. He said, "When I came home from work I found her, devastated, crushed by my infidelity. I could not bear to see her in such pain. I loved my wife, and I'd made a terrible decision without thinking about the consequences. Now I was face to face not only with the pain I'd caused her but with the possibility that I could lose my family. What had I been thinking?"

I've often shared with our church members something I call the five R's of resisting temptation. These are simple steps that can help you avoid succumbing to inappropriate desires.

1. **Remember who you are.** You are a child of God, a husband or wife, a parent, a friend. Is the behavior you are considering consistent with these roles?

2. **Recognize the consequences.** What will happen if your actions become known?

3. **Rededicate yourself to God.** When tempted, pause to pray and ask for God's grace and strength. Prayer is a way of pouring cold water on the fire of temptation.

4. **Reveal your struggle to a trusted friend.** Telling someone about it takes away the power of secret temptation and invites the other person's help in making you accountable.

5. **Remove yourself from the temptation.** Whether your struggle is with pornography, substance abuse, or the possibility of an affair, distancing yourself will usually help you resist. This might take the form of changing jobs, moving to a new location, or leaving behind a friendship. (If these actions seem extreme, keep in mind that, in the case of an affair, these are some of the very things that often result. Isn't it better to take action to save a marriage rather than wait until after the marriage is destroyed?)

As devastating as the threats of adultery, addiction, and abuse can be to a marriage, it is possible to work through them and survive. I have heard those stories as well. God can heal. God can deliver. God will show grace and mercy.

We are human. We make mistakes. We do things we shouldn't. But for those of us who are believers, the gospel brings good news. God offers second chances. God changes hearts and lives. God heals, mends, and resurrects broken things.

How can we begin the journey from brokenness to healing? We must request forgiveness from God and others. We must ask to be set free. Whether we are the abusers or the abused, we must look for God's help in loving those entrusted to our care.

Ours is a God who knows the struggles we face, who knows the allure of temptation, addiction, pornography, and adultery. Ours is a God who shows grace, who will forgive and heal us, who can repair broken relationships, and who, when repair is not possible, can offer us new beginnings. Our God gives hope to the hopeless.

REFLECT AND ENGAGE

Preparing for Temptation

Fantasies—you probably have a few of your own. It is natural to be attracted to others, and if your marriage is strong, these feelings about other people can remain merely that. But when cracks in your marital foundation form, those moments of appreciation toward or connection with someone else have the potential to seep in and fill a void that should not have been there. Instead, these moments plant a seed of "What if?" as you contemplate responding to a possible attraction and wandering down a dangerous road.

Acknowledging the inevitability of those moments when you notice the attractiveness of a friend's spouse or enjoy a laugh with a certain coworker, take time to think about what to do with unwelcome thoughts and feelings before they become a problem. Discuss the following questions together.

- What purpose do these feelings serve? Do they make you feel fun, young, desirable, and adventurous? Acknowledging the positive feelings can demystify the romance of them.
- Do you tell your spouse when moments like this occur? Do you want your spouse to tell you?
- In what areas of your relationship do you see potential "cracks in the foundation," through which an outside attraction could creep in? A lack of quality time together, boredom, or a point of discord could create these cracks that need to be avoided.

- What about situations when the "outside attraction" isn't even a real acquaintance — that is, when the problem is fantasy or even pornography? Do you share these attractions and temptations with your spouse? Are you in agreement as to limits on this behavior?

Pray Together

Dear God, when we fell in love and married, we could not imagine doing anything to hurt one another, and yet sometimes we end up doing just that. Help us to see the stumbling blocks while we are still far enough away to change course. Forgive us when we fail, and help us to forgive one another and find healing. Amen.

On Your Own

You may already have crossed some boundaries in situations like those described above. If you had a hard time discussing these issues and have something to confess to your spouse, consider talking to a trustworthy friend or your pastor.

If You're Single

Do you know couples whose marriages have been destroyed by adultery, pornography, addiction, or abuse? Did the couples come through these trials together or find separation necessary? How can you protect yourself against falling victim to these vices in the future?

5

CLOTHE, BEAR WITH, FORGIVE

As God's chosen ones, holy and beloved, clothe yourselves with compassion, kindness, humility, meekness, and patience. Bear with one another and, if anyone has a complaint against another, forgive each other; just as the Lord has forgiven you, so you also must forgive.

Colossians 3:12-13

A woman in our church sent me this riddle: What do you call an intelligent, good-looking, sensitive man? A rumor.

One of our staff sent me this joke: A man told his buddy he had taken his wife to Hawaii for their tenth anniversary.

"Wow, that's impressive!" the friend replied. "What will you do next year?"

The man said, "I'll go back and get her."

We may laugh at these jokes, but they capture the reality that men and women, husbands and wives, often frustrate, irritate, and exasperate one another. Because we're different from each other and are not always sensitive, we do sometimes feel like leaving our spouses in Hawaii and picking them up a year later!

In this chapter we'll consider some of the things men and women say that repel others from them. We'll also look at things we fight about. Finally, we'll examine three ideas from Scripture that are essential in making our love last.

How to Guarantee No Second Date

It turns out that the same social tool that can lead people to pornography and infidelity — the Internet — can also help men and women find love. Millions have used the Internet to meet potential romantic interests, and not a small number of these have led to marriage. Of the 927 single people taking our Love, Sex and Marriage survey, 47 percent said they had used an online dating service. Surprisingly, perhaps, most singles in their 20s had not used one. Fully two-thirds of those in their 30s and 40s had used them, and 57 percent of those in their 50s. Some 41 percent of those in their 60s, 10 percent of those in their 70s, and 7 percent of those in their 80s had used online dating services. These findings are consistent with what I've heard from couples whose weddings I have officiated, about half of whom met online.

"Met some nice people . . . and some real flakes."

About 20 to 30 percent of those we surveyed found the online dating experience to be great; they were currently dating someone they had found online. Another 30 to 40 percent were ambivalent, including a woman whose comment pretty much summed up that category: "Met some nice people and some real flakes." About 40 percent had bad experiences, ranging from "No one contacted me" to "Truly terrible."

We looked in Chapter 2 at the qualities men and women want in potential partners. In this chapter, we'll look at the things they *don't* want. This information should be valuable not only for singles, but for married people seeking to be the kind of spouse their partner would marry again. I want to know what women find distasteful in a man so I can avoid those things with my wife. As I noted in Chapter 2, I would like to be the man whom, if LaVon were dating today, she would fall in love with all over again.

When it came to online dating, the leading complaints in our survey from both men and women related to people being dishonest in the information they posted about themselves. A close second, expressed by women, was that many of the men were "just looking for sex." Our respondents said that, overall, honesty and a willingness to take things slowly were the keys to success.

Let's look more generally at things that short-circuit the dating process. We asked those taking our survey what kinds of behaviors or attitudes repelled them on the first date. In other words, what happened on the first date that guaranteed there would be no second date?

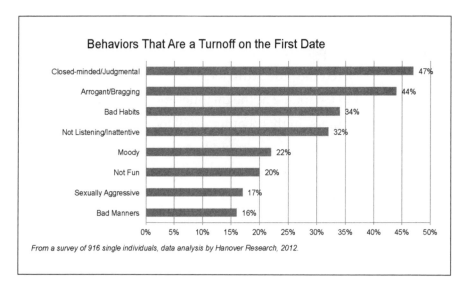

Behaviors That Are a Turnoff on the First Date

From a survey of 916 single individuals, data analysis by Hanover Research, 2012.

It turned out that, or this survey category, there were only minor differences between the responses of men and women. One difference for women was the inclusion of "inattentiveness": someone who wasn't paying attention on the first date wouldn't be getting a second. For men it was the inclusion of "moodiness" on the part of women: no second date for a woman who appeared to be moody.

The one trait that might need a little explanation is "bad habits." When the survey results came in, I took to Facebook to ask single men and women what constitutes a habit so bad that someone would lose a chance at a second date. I heard an earful, mostly from women. Bad hygiene and grooming were among the biggest turnoffs; failure to brush your teeth was a definite nonstarter, as was a lack of courtesy. Other no-no's included being rude to restaurant staff, being too picky, talking poorly about others or too much about yourself, and texting while on a date. Drinking too much and smoking were turnoffs to many.

What Irritates Us

What about those of us who make it through the dating process and get married? Which traits frustrate us about each other?

Let's start by admitting there are no perfect spouses.

We dealt in the last chapter with the big things that can kill a marriage, but what about small things that slowly pile up and ultimately can harm a marriage?

Let's start by admitting there are no perfect spouses. Each of us has quirks and idiosyncrasies. Each of us does things that irritate the other. Our survey asked married people what their spouses did that irritated them, and when I preached on the topic, our video team interviewed LaVon to get her answers to that very question. She laughed and said:

Occasionally, people will come up to me and say, "You are so lucky. You are married to Adam Hamilton." And you know, sometimes I just want to laugh, because he's just like any other guy. I mean, he has his faults. And he has the things that he does that frustrate me. We are very different people. And in fact I am lucky, but I think he's just as lucky.

He is somebody who I don't think has ever gotten anywhere on time. He runs late for everything. And I am a person who has to be fifteen minutes early to anywhere that I'm going.

He's also somebody who does not pick up anything after himself. I guess maybe that's true for a lot of men. But socks do fall where they are taken off and coats have been laid where they're taken off. I have a spot in our house that, about once a week, I'll gather all of his stuff up and just pile it there. Sometimes it gets to be a pretty big pile. He'll eventually go through it. But at least it's out of my sight.

I got off easy in that interview! I do, or fail to do, lots of other things that I know frustrate her.

Along those lines, in our survey we asked married women, "What one thing would you change about your spouse if you could?" Here were their top five answers:

Married Women
1. I wish he would listen to me.
2. I want him to share his feelings with me.
3. I wish he weren't so short-tempered.
4. I'd like him to help me around the house.
5. I wish he weren't so negative.

LaVon frequently tells me I'm not listening, and I always think, *Yes, I am!* One night when we were having supper, she said she wasn't feeling well. Knowing how important it is to her that I listen, I tried to express concern. I nodded and sympathized and expressed empathy and concern. "I'm so sorry," I said, and asked if there was anything I could do. I finished with, "I hope you get to feeling better." I was proud of myself for being Mr. Sensitivity.

We watched TV for a while, and after she'd gotten ready for bed, it was time to show that I remembered she wasn't feeling well and to score some points while I was at it. The trouble was, I couldn't remember if it was her head or her stomach that hurt. I decided it had been her head and asked, "Is your headache gone?"

"Nice try," she said, "but it was my stomach, and it's doing fine now."

It's clear that my definition of paying attention and hers aren't identical. I think that's a difference between men and women: We have different ways of listening. Somehow my brain doesn't retain all the information she transmits to me. Meanwhile, LaVon is thinking, *If you really loved me, you'd remember what I was feeling. You wouldn't have to guess.* The message I sent that night was that, while I pretended to care, I didn't really care or I would have remembered.

I think many guys are somewhat like me. Even when we try, we don't always catch all the details. That's not an excuse; it's the way we are.

Let's look at the top five things men in our survey told us they would change about their wives:

Married Men

1. I wish she were more interested in sexual intimacy.
2. I would like her to nag me less.
3. I wish she wouldn't overreact.
4. I would like her to be less negative.
5. I wish she wouldn't criticize me so much.

The two lists showed some interesting contrasts. Women wanted more meaningful communication; men wanted more sexual intimacy. Women needed assurance that men were listening and communicating; men needed physical demonstrations of love and affection. Women responded poorly to short tempers; men responded poorly to criticism and overreaction. Both disliked negativity.

Negativity seems to come more naturally at home.

There seemed to be some consistent patterns in the actions and reactions of married couples in our survey. Interestingly, in many cases these behaviors weren't carried into the workplace or into friendships, but they showed up in dealings at home.

I know, for instance, as a leader at The Church of the Resurrection, that I need to give five words of encouragement with every one word of constructive criticism. This "rule of five" is a key to effectively leading, motivating, and encouraging people in the workplace. But often I don't remember to do this at home, instead going straight into constructive criticism, which often doesn't sound very constructive.

Negativity seems to come more naturally at home, where we let our guard down. We do it with our spouses and our kids. Your child shows you a report card with two A's, three B's and a C. What are you most likely to talk about? The C, of course. It seems that that's how we're wired. At home we don't structure our comments positively, as we generally try to do at work. And yet we know that people, our families included, respond much better to positive, optimistic, and hopeful comments than to negative ones. We forget that a positive spirit is vital in order for people to thrive, at work, and at home.

Given the choice between being married to someone who is negative all the time and someone who at least part of the time is positive and hopeful, most of us would choose to be around the spouse with hope. That's why we need to be the spouse with hope.

Here's something else from the workplace that we might apply at home: an annual marriage review. In researching the idea I found an article in *Psychology Today* by psychologist Sam Margulies, who described it well. Most marriages, he said, don't fall apart suddenly from one of the big issues we dealt with earlier—addiction, abuse, adultery. Instead, they fall apart in a long, slow slide as couples allow small issues to get bigger and bigger until they collapse of their own weight.

What would happen, he wrote, if we addressed those small issues early on instead of letting them grow? It's how we strive to handle business problems; why not do the same thing in our marriages? At our church, for example, we've occasionally had employees who were good people trying to do good things but weren't quite hitting the mark. When we didn't address those issues early on, they got worse and worse until finally the situation blew up. That's exactly what happens in many marriages. Instead of talking about small problems in a constructive way, we allow them to build up until they reach a tipping point.

Margulies laid out what he called the Annual Marriage Performance Review. It uses a form that lets you and your mate evaluate yourselves and each other. You add up the scores and see what you're doing well and what you're not doing well.[21]

Really? You never disagree about anything?

That's exactly how it works with my own job at The Church of the Resurrection. My annual performance review has several components. I do a self-evaluation. Other people evaluate me. Then our personnel committee (in United Methodist Churches this is usually called the Staff Parish Committee) brings those two evaluations together so we can see what I'm doing well and what I need to improve on. Based on the review, each year we set a couple of goals with specific and measurable outcomes. It's an approach that helps me improve and meet the needs of our church. Why not bring the same sensible process to my marriage?

The Annual Marriage Performance Review asks, "In the past year, how have I performed on the following behaviors?" It allows answers from 1 to 5, with 1 being really well and 5 being really badly. The statements include:

- I've been sensitive to your sexual needs.
- I have listened well when you tell me something that is important to you.
- On most days I'm reasonably cheerful.

- I have done my share of the household chores.
- I spend enough time with the children.

There are many other questions, but you get the idea. When you're finished, you look for places that are most in need of improvement. You evaluate yourself, your mate evaluates you, and you bring those evaluations together and set some goals. Too often, though, instead of sitting down and talking through problems, married couples avoid conflict until the situation blows up.

How Frequently We Fight

I often remind couples that conflict is a normal and healthy part of life. When I meet with couples before they get married, during their last session of premarital counseling I ask, "What do you fight about?" The couples I worry most about are those who say, "Oh, we never fight."

Really? You never disagree about anything? If you never fight, if neither of you ever says, "I don't like what you did there" or "I don't agree with that," then somewhere someone isn't being fully honest. Couples are going to clash. That's just normal.

Keep in mind that frequency of conflict is no indicator of the happiness or success of a marriage. There are couples who fight only once a year, but their fighting is so destructive and painful that their relationship is extremely unhealthy. There are other couples who get into some sort of tiff pretty much every day, but they resolve those skirmishes in a healthy way, so that ultimately they are able to maintain a great relationship.

With that in mind, we asked on our survey how often married people fought with their spouses. Here is what they told us:

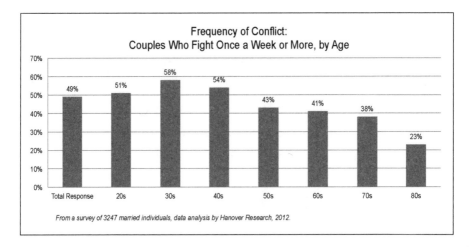

Frequency of Conflict:
Couples Who Fight Once a Week or More, by Age

From a survey of 3247 married individuals, data analysis by Hanover Research, 2012.

Note that after the conflict peaked in the 30s, the percentage of married people who fought appeared to decrease in each decade starting in the 40s. This trend seemed to indicate that if you can hang in there through your 30s, you can probably expect less conflict as you grow older. In our case, after thirty years of marriage, the amount of conflict LaVon and I experience has gone down dramatically. We still have spats sometimes and get really angry with each other, but it doesn't happen often, and in general the frequency and intensity of our fights has gone way down. We blow off some steam now and then, and before long one of us says, "I shouldn't have said that. I'm really sorry." And the other will say, "Yeah, me too. I love you." And we're done.

Why do LaVon and I have less major conflict as we grow older? I suspect there are several reasons. As each decade goes by, we've learned more about the likes, dislikes, and needs of the other.

After our kids grew up there was a bit less stress. We're financially better off than we were in the early years of our marriage. We're also maturing. Things that used to bother me just really don't bother me much anymore. I think, *It's not that big a deal. Let it go.* LaVon does the same. We're both better spouses than we were in the early years. She is more attentive to my needs, and I think I am more attentive to hers. We are more caring, loving, and patient today than when we first married. That's how it is supposed to be. In the Christian spiritual life we call this sanctification, a process by which the Holy Spirit perfects us over time. We're meant to see more fruit of the Spirit in our lives and to become more Christlike as we continue on our spiritual journeys.

I want you to hear this:
You are normal.

The numbers from our survey on the subject of conflict tell me that if we're patient, if we can get past the "If I were only married to someone else" kind of thinking, the amount of conflict is likely to go down over time, and our stress levels should go down as well. So don't give up! Keep pressing on. Keep working on your relationship, allowing time to grow spiritually and emotionally.

What We Fight About

As we work toward greater marital harmony, let's remember what we learned earlier in the book. Each bit of conflict is a withdrawal from our mate's love bank, and the more serious our conflicts become, the more likely they are to threaten our marriage.

With that reminder, let's look at what we actually fight about, keeping in mind that men and women see things differently. We asked the married people who took our survey to tell us what they fought about with their spouses, and this is what they told us:

Men: What We Fight About with Our Wives

1. Communication/failure to listen
2. Money/finances
3. Feeling unappreciated
4. Sex
5. Household responsibilities/inattentive to my needs

Women: What We Fight About with Our Husbands

1. Communication/failure to listen
2. Money/finances
3. Feeling unappreciated
4. Household responsibilities
5. Children

On this topic the lists were nearly identical, the only difference of substance being that men perceived more conflicts about sex than women perceived. (For men, "children" finished a close sixth.)

Most of us who are married will recognize at least something on these lists that we fight about with some regularity. If that's true for you, I want you to hear this: *You are normal.* Normal people have conflicts over these things.

We sometimes feel that the other isn't listening or doesn't appreciate us. We fight over how to spend money. We feel that the other is more (or less) interested in sex than we are and doesn't help around the house as much as we'd like. We sometimes think, *If I could only change partners, I wouldn't fight about these things.* Yes, you would! These are things we routinely fight about because we are *human*. We see the world in different ways and have different ideas about how to resolve our conflicts.

What Paul Tells Us

So, if conflicts are inevitable, if you're pretty much guaranteed to irritate each other now and then, how do you live together? What do you do to make a marriage work?

The truth is that that question could be asked about any relationship. How do you make it work with your best friend? Friends aren't perfect either. They're going to hurt your feelings; you're going to hurt theirs. The two of you will see the world differently.

This is where the words of the apostle Paul come into play. The Scripture passage at the beginning of this chapter is one I read at every single wedding I officiate — more than three hundred of them at this point. I do so because what Paul says here is so foundational to any marriage — or any relationship. Let's read it again:

119

As God's chosen ones, holy and beloved, clothe yourselves with compassion, kindness, humility, meekness, and patience. Bear with one another and, if anyone has a complaint against another, forgive each other; just as the Lord has forgiven you, so you also must forgive. (Colossians 3:12-13)

Let's start where Paul started, with the idea of clothing yourself. Attitude is like clothing. It's something people can see and pick up on right away when they're in your presence.

Make sure, says Paul, that the first things people notice when they come in contact with you are virtues. They should pick up on your kindness and compassion, your gentleness and humility and patience. These aren't things we wear naturally. If they were, Paul wouldn't need to remind us. These are attitudes we have to work at.

I often find that it's easier to practice these virtues with church members or friends than it is with my wife, and yet she is the one person whom I've made a lifelong covenant to love! She is the one person God is most counting on me to practice them with.

How do we go about clothing ourselves in these virtues? The first step is to make a decision that it's important to God and to you. You might even write these verses down and place them where you'll see them every day — for instance, on the mirror where you brush your teeth. Whenever you see the verses, pray them. Say, "Lord, I'm grateful to be one of your chosen ones. I'm holy and beloved to you. Please help me to be more compassionate. Help me to demonstrate greater kindness to the people who are close to me. I want to walk with humility. Please help me to consider the needs of others before my own. Help me to be gentle and meek. And, Lord, please teach me patience!"

When I pray in this way, the very act causes me to internalize these virtues. As with all the Bible's virtues, they are a by-product of the Holy Spirit's work in our lives. In Galatians 5:22 Paul calls them the "fruit of the spirit." He says, in essence, that when we allow God's Holy Spirit to work inside of us, these virtues are more manifest in our lives, which is why there is a strong connection between faith and successful relationships. It's not a guarantee, but as we grow in faith—and especially as two people grow *together* in faith—we find that over time we become kinder, gentler, more patient, and more compassionate toward one another, showing a greater concern for the other's needs rather than our own.

Victoria's Secret offers clothing meant to spice up a relationship. Yet think how much more the clothing described by Paul can enrich your relationship. If you want your love to last, then check out the closetful of attributes listed in this passage. When two people are compassionate toward one another—kind and gentle, humble and patient—they form a love bond that can't be broken. That's what Paul offers us here.

Then, ever the realist, Paul goes on to say, "Bear with one another" (Colossians 3:13). In another translation he asks us to be "longsuffering" (v. 12 NKJV). Why, after listing all the ways we can bless each other, does Paul have to write these words?

Because he recognizes that sometimes we fall short. We're going to irritate each other, so we'll need to put up with each other.

LaVon has learned to live with me, and I with her. She realizes that, no matter how hard I try, some of the traits that have annoyed her since the beginning of our marriage aren't likely to change. She wishes I worked out more, that I could dance without stepping on her feet, that I was more lighthearted. Sometimes she wishes I had a job that gave me weekends off and a bit more privacy. LaVon and I have both learned, and are still learning, to bear with one another.

John Gottman, the marriage expert who wrote *The Seven Principles for Making Marriage Work*, gives us another word for that attitude: acceptance. According to Gottman, accepting your partner's personality is an important key to conflict resolution, which means it's essential to making marriage work.[22] At some point you say to yourself, *You know what? I love her even though she's not perfect. I know all her negatives, but I still choose to love her because the positives compensate for them.*

Of course, there are some things people can't put up with. We've talked about adultery, abuse, and addiction, issues so painful they can be dealbreakers. In addition, there are smaller issues. These are things that cause real pain and require a measure of grace to be dealt with. If we are to move beyond them, there are six words that may be as important as any spoken in a marriage, perhaps even more important than "I love you." The six words are: "I am sorry" and "I forgive you." If you're unable to say those words, you have no chance of making a friendship, a family relationship, or a marriage last. It's that simple.

Paul puts it this way: "If anyone has a complaint against another, forgive each other; just as the Lord has forgiven you, so you also must forgive" (Colossians 3:13b). What a challenge—to forgive as Jesus forgave us. In Luke's Gospel we are given a powerful picture of Jesus hanging on the cross, looking down upon the Pharisees and Romans who hung him there. "Father, forgive them," he said, "for they do not know what they are doing" (Luke 23:34). Earlier, in teaching us to pray, Jesus said, "Forgive us our debts, as we also have forgiven our debtors" (Matthew 6:12). Forgiveness is a powerful tool, an antidote to pain in our lives.

The Grace of God

Repentance and forgiveness set two people free: the one who has been hurt and the one who has done the hurting. These two actions heal relationships in ways we can hardly fathom. But there's one case in which Jesus acknowledged that even repentance and forgiveness may not always heal a relationship, and that is adultery.

Jesus noted that this breach of the marriage covenant is so traumatic that people may need to end the marriage over it. It is an exception to the rule that marriage is for life. In Matthew 5:32 Jesus said, "But I say to you that whoever divorces his wife except for sexual unfaithfulness forces her to commit adultery" (CEB). Note, however, that Jesus didn't say you have to divorce. He just said there's permission to do so in the wake of infidelity. I have known many people whose marriages survived infidelity, and it was in large part because they were able to practice repentance and forgiveness.

"I choose to forgive in the morning and I choose to forgive at the end of the day."

One woman whose husband had been unfaithful wrote to me and said, "The one thing that kept me going was something I heard in a previous sermon of yours: 'Choose to forgive every day the way Jesus has forgiven us daily for our own sins.'"

She said the thought of having to forgive all at once was overwhelming. "So instead," she said, "I choose to forgive in the morning and I choose to forgive at the end of the day. It doesn't feel quite as overwhelming if it goes along with the idea of taking 'one day at a time.' If I hadn't have thought of it this way, our marriage would not have survived. But instead, today our marriage is stronger than it has ever been before."

That is a miracle, really. It's something that doesn't happen except by the grace of God, working in our lives to heal the part that is broken, taking it out of the ashes and making it into something more beautiful than it was before. This woman and her husband are living proof that grace is possible in the hardest of situations.

God's grace, when coupled with the power of repentance and forgiveness, has a profound ability to heal. I mention the following story as a way of illustrating the healing power of forgiveness.

On July 4, 2011, eleven-year-old Blair Lane was playing with friends in the backyard of her uncle's house on Riss Lake near Parkville, Missouri. A thousand feet away, fifty-year-old Aaron Sullivan was celebrating Independence Day with his friends at an apartment complex. Sullivan decided to fire a few rounds of his pistol into the lake, and he then handed the gun to his friends, who did the same. One of the bullets ricocheted off the water, or something in the water, and traveled a thousand feet, striking young Blair in the neck. She died the next day.

By all accounts, Sullivan was a good guy who, with a moment's thoughtlessness, ended a life. He was charged with manslaughter and pleaded guilty, though it was uncertain whose bullet had done the damage. He made no excuses, telling the judge how foolish he had been and how terribly sorry he was. At the sentencing hearing, he turned to the family and said, "I am so sorry. I wish I could take it back. I wish it had never happened. I hope you can find it in your heart to forgive me." He was sentenced to three years in prison.

As Sullivan walked out of the courtroom, Blair's father, Jason Lane, called out to him. He walked toward him, stretched out his hand, and whispered something in his ear. The two men embraced. A photographer for *The Kansas City Star* captured the moment, and the photo was in the paper the next day. A reporter asked Jason Lane what he had said to Aaron Sullivan. Jason said, "I forgave him. I introduced myself and forgave him."[23]

As I read that story I thought, *If it's possible for a father to forgive the man who killed his daughter, what is there in my marriage that I cannot forgive?*

When the two men embraced, there was liberation for both of them — for Jason Lane from a lifetime of bitterness, and for Aaron Sullivan from a lifetime of guilt. Forgiveness has the power to heal. It has the power to set us free. And it's absolutely essential to making love last.

Every one of us has hurt someone close to us. We've said things we shouldn't have said. We've done things we shouldn't have done. Are there things you've done for which you need to be forgiven? Are you carrying around bitterness because you haven't forgiven someone else? In either case, approach God. You might ask, "Lord, give me the strength to ask forgiveness" or "Lord, help me to forgive." In earnestly repenting and in extending grace, you will find the healing power of God at work in your life.

God knows the wounds we have inflicted on each other. He knows the bitterness and resentment that can build up in any marriage. He offers us the tools to overcome those feelings, along with the grace to heal us, so we may enjoy marriage as the blessing it was designed to be.

REFLECT AND ENGAGE

Marriage Performance Review

John Gottman, the marriage expert who wrote *The Seven Principles for Making Marriage Work*, talks about what he calls the "Four Horsemen of the Apocalypse": criticism, defensiveness, contempt, and stonewalling. While these negative behaviors can creep into any marriage, the couples whose relationships more likely to last a lifetime are those who are able to recognize and remedy these behaviors, not allowing them to take root.[24]

All of us grapple with a few of these negative behaviors and can testify as to their destructive nature and the frustrating cycle they can cause. Negativity, whether in the form of nagging, criticism, a short temper, or contemptuous mannerisms such as eye rolling, can cause an energy sinkhole in a marriage that drains a love tank fast.

The "rule of five" that was mentioned in the chapter—the five positive interactions it takes to balance out one negative interaction—is one way to remind yourself to increase your expressions of love and affirmation, but how do we rein in our negative actions in general? One way is simply to be more aware, and to help one another be more aware, in a calm, nonthreatening way.

To create a marriage performance review such as the one mentioned in the chapter, begin by listing together five to ten behaviors you each want to work on, to improve how you already show love in the ways your partner desires and to control negative behaviors to which you are prone. Consider the following questions to help you make a list for each of you, and to perform an initial assessment when you are done.

- In what ways has your partner indicated he or she would like you to show your love? (Look back to the "Wish List" activity from Chapter 2 if you need reminders.) What other positive actions do you want to use in tracking your performance?
- What negative behaviors do you need to work on? Discuss these calmly together in a collaborative manner, without being critical or accusatory. Phrase these items on your list in a positive way.
- To make an initial assessment, rate yourselves on each item from 1 to 5, then trade and let your partner evaluate you while you evaluate him or her. Compare how you rated yourself with how well your spouse thinks you are doing on each item, and discuss the issue without getting defensive. Set goals for improvement in problem areas.
- Plan to revisit your performance reviews in six months or a year. Discuss how each of you has improved, and add anything to the list that you want to work on going forward.

Pray Together

Dear God, it is so hard to admit my own faults, and even harder to break negative habits that hurt my spouse and our marriage. Help me to be humble enough to hear my partner's concerns and kind enough to share mine in constructive ways. Thank you for your endless grace that enables us to put the past behind us and do better in the future. Amen.

On Your Own

How did it feel to put your most challenging behaviors on paper and to have your spouse make you aware of something you did not think of as a problem? How did you respond? Pray and reflect on your behaviors, seeking the humility and respect for your partner's feelings to work on the things that trouble your spouse, whether or not you agree on the severity of the issue.

If You're Single

While you're not working right now on being a better spouse, you can always work on being a better person and follower of Christ. Make a list of character traits and behaviors you strive for. Rate yourself on these things, noting elements that are particularly challenging for you, and make a plan to improve in these areas to refine your character toward the person you want to be.

6

A LOVE THAT LASTS

Above all, clothe yourselves with love, which binds everything together in perfect harmony. And let the peace of Christ rule in your hearts, to which indeed you were called in the one body. And be thankful.

Colossians 3:14-15

Helen hadn't seen her friend Ruth in years, as the two women had lived in different states for decades. So when Helen came to town, she was looking forward to an evening with Ruth and her husband of more than 60 years. Upon arriving, Helen was struck by the way Ruth spoke to her husband, calling him "Honey," "Sweetheart," "Darling," or often simply "My Love."

Helen finally told Ruth, "I think it's wonderful that you speak to your husband in such loving terms after all these years."

Ruth replied, "To tell you the truth, his name slipped my mind about ten years ago, and I'm scared to ask the old crank what it is!"

The story seems appropriate as we bring this book to a close, focusing on the seasons of marriage and what it takes to share a love that lasts a lifetime.

Why don't more marriages last? Why can't more couples celebrate fifty or sixty years as husband and wife? What makes married love so difficult? As we consider the challenges to marriage and analyze some tools and tactics for dealing with them, let's look at the kind of marriage we're talking about, the kind that does last a lifetime.

When I meet couples who have been married more than fifty years, I usually ask this question: "What does it take to stay married so long?" The answer is virtually always "perseverance" or "commitment." They go on to talk about other factors, but the bottom line is always a simple willingness to stick it out. None of them says it's easy. They talk about hard times, periods when they were frustrated or didn't feel love for each other. Every relationship faces such times, they say, and only a real dedication to the underlying covenant will keep a couple together. Clearly, for these couples marriage is much more than a piece of paper.

It's also worth noting that virtually every couple with that kind of married longevity says they're glad they stayed together.

The Seasons of Marriage

As we analyzed responses from the 3,856 married people who took our Love, Sex, and Marriage survey, we found that their experiences seemed to line up with national surveys regarding married couples at various stages in their lives. One of the questions we asked in the survey was: "Are you happy and fulfilled in your marriage?"

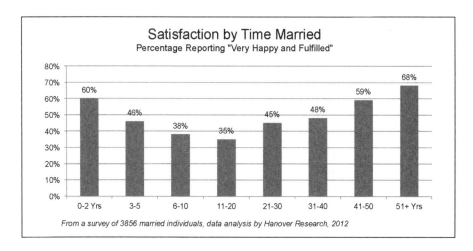

Satisfaction by Time Married
Percentage Reporting "Very Happy and Fulfilled"

From a survey of 3856 married individuals, data analysis by Hanover Research, 2012

As you can see, the responses clearly were related to the length of time the respondents had been married. Among people who had been married for two years or less, for instance, about 60 percent reported being very happy and fulfilled. Between two and five years, that figure dropped to 46 percent. From six to ten years it was 38 percent, and from eleven to twenty years it fell even further.

But then, beginning at twenty-one years, the percentage rose dramatically, and those who had been married longer than fifty years reported being happier than the newlyweds!

It's a fascinating emotional roadmap, and it's consistent with our survey information collected from the 1300 respondents who had been divorced. We asked how long they had been married when they split up, and the answers were consistent with the happiness survey.

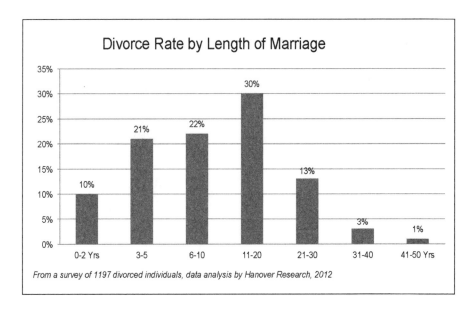

From a survey of 1197 divorced individuals, data analysis by Hanover Research, 2012

We see a low divorce rate in the first two years, then a huge rise in the divorce rate from three to five years and a further rise from six to ten years. The divorce rate is high but not quite as high from eleven to twenty years, then it drops off after twenty years and again at thirty years. After forty years of marriage, the divorce rate drops precipitously.

Let's consider what's happening and why. The average person we surveyed was married at age twenty-eight, so for this group of people the period when the most divorces occur — between two and ten years of marriage — began at age thirty.

What's going on in a couple's early thirties that seems so problematic for marriage? First, we stop courting and doing those magical things we did before marriage and during the first two years afterward. We don't go on as many dates. We don't have those deep learn-about-each-other talks as often. We don't treat each other as special. The Neil Diamond/Barbra Streisand song had it right: "You don't bring me flowers/You don't sing me love songs anymore."[25] Somewhere along the line we change those habits. We stop doing the things we should have been doing all along.

It happens in the spiritual realm as well. In Revelation 2:4-5, when speaking to one of the churches being addressed, Jesus says, in effect, "You've lost your first love. Your spiritual passion is gone. So go back and do the things you did at first when you began to follow me, and you'll reclaim your spiritual passion."

Do the things you did at first. This is a straightforward method for dealing with the problems that beset so many marriages: look honestly at the things you've stopped doing, and start doing them again.

In addition to this decline in habits, another factor that affects marriage in our early thirties is that our careers heat up. We're trying to make a name for ourselves. We're working overtime to pay the bills and perhaps move up the ladder. We're going in a hundred directions at once.

When LaVon and I were in our 30s, the church had just moved into our first building. In one week we more than doubled in size, from 500 to 1200 people in worship. We began launching capital campaigns. All of a sudden, I was running like crazy. I'd go home, wolf down a quick dinner, and go back for a meeting. In fact, at one point I was in a meeting every single night for two weeks. Finally LaVon said, "This is not working."

I said, "Honey, don't worry. I'll be home tonight. I have a meeting, but I'll leave it early. If you can hold dinner, I'll be home."

She held dinner. The meeting dragged on and on. The conversation was important enough that I didn't feel I could step out. This was well before text messaging, so there was no way I could tell LaVon what was happening. It was 7:30, then 8:00, then 8:30, then 9:00. Finally, at 9:15, the meeting ended.

We lived right behind the church, and when I came around the corner and saw the house, I knew I was in trouble. There wasn't a light on anywhere. LaVon had put the kids to bed. The house was dark and silent.

"You're overdrawn at the love bank, buddy. Your account is empty."

I went up the stairs. The French doors leading into the bedroom were shut, and my pillow was on the floor outside. It was her way of saying, "You're overdrawn at the love bank, buddy. Your account is empty."

I stood at the door and groveled for a while. Finally she let me in, but I knew things would have to change.

That scenario plays out in so many marriages. Sometimes there are two careers, and both husband and wife have those kinds of schedules. The toll taken by work can be enormous.

Children and Early Marriage

Declining habits and difficult work schedules are important reasons why couples in their early thirties seem to have problems, but I don't think they are the primary reasons. There's an even bigger factor at work in derailing happiness for young married couples: kids.

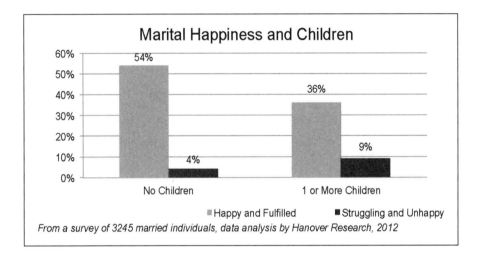

Turning back to our Love, Sex, and Marriage survey, we found that couples who had children reported that they were happy and fulfilled 36 percent of the time. Couples with no children in the home reported happy and fulfilled marriages 54 percent of the time. That is a huge statistical difference, and it aligns with national numbers.

It's important to note here that there is another side to the equation: Couples with children reported more of a sense of meaning and purpose in their lives than those without. But happiness suffered.

I've experienced that tradeoff. There is tremendous joy in having kids. Other than my walk with Christ, the greatest joy I have ever had was being a dad. I would catch myself thinking,

I can't believe I get to be a daddy, to hold this child in my arms and experience fatherhood. Being a parent is an awesome feeling, but it takes a toll on a marriage. If only someone had told me that!

LaVon and I had our first child while I was in seminary at Southern Methodist University in Dallas. She was working full time. I was earning my master's degree and working almost full-time. It would be difficult to convey just how much we loved that child. The experience of holding Danielle in my arms was amazing. I didn't know I could love another human being as much as I loved her, and still do. It was different from my love for LaVon. I believe I loved her even *more* than I loved LaVon, and LaVon loved her more than she loved me. Danielle absolutely stole our hearts.

I remember lying there one Saturday morning, looking across the bed at LaVon and realizing I didn't love her anymore.

But this little person needed attention — lots of attention, from two people who were working and busy and a little stressed. She had colic. She had ear infections. She would wake in the middle of the night and cry her little heart out. Every spare bit of attention we had went toward her, leaving nothing for each other. There was no time to go out on dates. There was no time to be intimate. There was no time even to communicate. It was work, school, and take care of the baby.

When Danielle was about six months old, I remember lying there one Saturday morning, looking across the bed at LaVon and realizing I didn't love her anymore. That feeling terrified me. I remember thinking, *What does this mean?*

Now, I was a trouper. I was in it for the long haul. I was going to treat her with love, but I didn't feel love. I didn't feel anything. I told two of my buddies, "I guess this is what they mean when they talk about the honeymoon being over." And I thought, like so many people in that situation think, that it was going to be that way forever. I thought the spark, the magic, the passion would never return. I would spend the rest of my life going through the motions. It was a depressing thought. And I learned that LaVon felt the same way.

One night three or four months later, I was working late on a paper. LaVon had already gone to bed. As I worked, I found myself grieving the loss of the love we had felt. And then I felt this nudging, which I usually take to be the work of the Holy Spirit, and I heard, *Get up and go buy her flowers.*

I don't think so, I thought.

Get up and buy her flowers.

I heard it three times.

Fine, I thought. I pulled on my sweat pants, got in the car and drove to the 24-hour grocery down the road. I got a dozen flowers and walked to the cash register. As I stood in line I felt this little nudge.

Go get her a card.

Okay, fine. I got a card, got back in line, paid for both and went home.

I thought, *What can I write on this card? Thanks for nothing?*

As bad as it sounds, that was what I thought. All the magic had been drained from our relationship. Then I felt another nudge.

Bless her with your words.

What can I say, I thought, *that could bless her and still be true?*

Slowly, the words began forming.

Dear LaVon, thank you for being such a great mom to Danielle.

And then, *Thank you for working full-time so that I can go to seminary. Thank you for carrying more than your share of the load around the house.*

It was getting easier.

Thank you for putting up with me when I'm a jerk. Thank you for the way you smiled at me the other day and how your eyes lit up.

You *do* love until you *feel* love.

Each phrase, each thought, came a little more readily to my mind and to my pen, until by the time I had finished writing that note, I felt something I hadn't felt in a year—a hint of the love I had lost. I began getting a sense of what I was supposed to do. It was then that I discovered the mission of marriage. It wasn't for me to feel happy and in love. The mission was for me to bless my wife. And so I began trying to find little ways that I could bless her. And she began to do the same for me. Three or four months later, I was lying in bed one Saturday morning, and I looked over at her and thought, *I am so in love with you.*

I have tried to carry the lessons I learned in that season of doubt and renewal into everything I do as a preacher and pastor.

Called to Do Love

We have this idea that first you fall in love, and then it follows naturally that you do loving things. But in marriage it works the opposite way. First you do loving things, because as a Christian and a married person you're called to do them. Then, when you persistently do loving things toward somebody, eventually you feel the love again. You *do* love until you *feel* love.

That was one of the most important things I learned in the early years of my marriage. Love is not a feeling; it is the way I live and act toward another human being, whether I feel like it or not. When it is difficult to feel love, the trick is to hold on to the knowledge that it will get better and not to do anything stupid in the meantime.

Love is a dance, and part of what LaVon and I did as young parents was learn to dance with a third person, a precious little person. Then we had another child, Rebecca, and learned to dance with four. The changes were difficult, but we found joy in all of them. By the time Danielle and Rebecca were in middle school, we had found our sea legs. And the four of us danced for eighteen years.

Then Danielle moved away, and we entered the second great period of trial for many marriages: that time when the kids begin moving out. People told me how hard it would be, but still I was not prepared. LaVon and I entered the second highly vulnerable period of our marriage. We experienced an intense grief when Danielle left. Rebecca then had both of us to herself, and all of us tried to figure out the new dynamics of life with just three

141

of us in the home. I think LaVon was struggling a bit with who she was at that point, since the kids were so much a part of her identity. I didn't feel that as much. I just felt grief.

To further complicate matters, Rebecca became a real pill during her senior year in high school. The good news? It would be easier to say goodbye when she moved away! In the meantime, though, it added new difficulties to what her mom and I were going through. It helped stir conflicting emotions as LaVon and I anticipated the grief that would come when both of our children were gone. We wondered how our marriage was going to work when we weren't Mommy and Daddy anymore.

When Rebecca finally moved out, we went through a disorienting period that lasted three years. I kept trying to do the things that had helped when I was twenty-two, and of course they just didn't work anymore.

"How do you fix this?" I asked myself. I had no idea what to do. LaVon felt the same way. After dancing as four, then three, we had to learn to dance again as two. There were moments when I thought, I can't do this for the next fifty years. LaVon and I struggled, and I do mean struggled. There were times when I wasn't sure our marriage would survive.

But if you learn the lessons of the early years, you remember perseverance and commitment. You hang in there. If somebody had just told me, "Look, it's going to get a lot better in about six months," I might have had an easier time, but no one said anything. That's why I'm telling you now — it's like that for almost everybody.

This disorienting phase of life is sometimes accompanied by other challenges. The timing coincides with the onset of menopause for some women. For men and women, wrinkles, gray and thinning hair, and occasionally stalled careers can lead to a feeling that life is passing us by. Our sex lives may seem boring. The romance or excitement we felt when we were younger may have been lost in the midst of rearing children. We may long for excitement. In this time of life we are particularly vulnerable to developing feelings for someone else, someone who makes us feel special or makes our heart beat faster. For so many people who haven't effectively dealt with the challenges in their marriage, who don't understand that midlife disorientation is only temporary, who are unwilling to invest time and energy in improving their marriage, they succumb to temptation during this difficult phase, or they slowly drift apart.

One look at divorce statistics tells us that many marriages simply don't make it. Some marriages have such serious problems that they're doomed under any circumstances, but in many cases it's a matter of someone who doesn't understand the normal trials and cycles of marriage and isn't prepared for them. It's about a spouse who throws in the towel rather than hanging in there until it gets better.

I can tell you that today, a few years after our youngest moved away, LaVon and I are more in love than we've ever been. It took a while before we were back in balance again, but we got there. The relationship we used to have has had a chance to resurface. We can do things we couldn't do when we had kids. Once again she's my best friend, and I think I'm her best friend. I'm so glad that through the seasons when it was difficult, neither of us gave up.

Of course, that's my marriage, not yours. Your journey is unique and unpredictable; the one thing I can say for sure is that there will be challenges. The key is remembering to hold on tight. Love until you feel it. Listen and try to understand. And realize that counseling and the support of others can be very helpful.

There is one last season that offers its own set of challenges. For most of us it's not as serious as those we've discussed so far, but for some people it's just as troublesome in its own way. I'm speaking of retirement.

A quick review of some statistics from our survey will help set the stage here: The percentage of married people who fight at least once a week. As we've seen before, that number remains pretty steady for the first twenty years of marriage, with a little over 50 percent of couples reporting weekly fights. The percentage drops once the kids move out of the house. But then, among those who have been married for thirty-five to fifty years, the percentage of those who fight at least once a week rises and peaks.

Couples learn to dance as a twosome again once the kids are gone, but at first, since one or both are still working, they only deal with each other during evenings and weekends. Then, with retirement, couples often spend a lot more time together, and conflicts arise. Men especially can face an identity crisis at this point. They can't figure out who they are now that they're no longer identified with a job or career. During this season, couples must help each other discover new sources of meaning and purpose.

Fortunately, this period doesn't seem to last too long, and in a matter of months or a year, the joy returns to the relationship.

The Best Is Yet to Be

In the Scripture that opens this chapter, which completes the passage from Colossians that I read at every wedding I officiate, Paul closes with some fundamental truths to keep in mind as we consider the different seasons of marriage.

Paul tells us that the way to make marriage work is to clothe ourselves with love. Here the Greek term for love is *agape*, and it's an important word. As mentioned before, there are multiple words for love in Greek. Some have to do with feelings and emotions, with romance as most of us conceive it. But that's not the word Paul uses here. He can't command us to feel the emotion of love or to bask in romance. But he can tell us to exhibit a love that seeks to bless the other person, to build up, to encourage. He can urge us toward a love that seeks the other person's best, with nothing expected in return. When we clothe ourselves in this kind of selfless love—when I'm always seeking your best, and you're always seeking mine—then love can work, even when we don't feel it.

When asked about the most important thing God wants of us, Jesus said, "You shall love the Lord your God with all your heart, and with all your soul, and with all your mind" and "You shall love your neighbor as yourself" (Matthew 22:37, 39). In this passage Jesus wasn't talking about feelings. He was talking about *agape* love, self-giving love. And while we're looking at words, "your neighbor" is not just the person who lives next door. Your neighbor is also the person who sleeps next to you at night, this person you've been called to love as you love yourself.

Part of the challenge is that some of us don't love ourselves, which makes it hard to love someone else. I need to discover the love of God and in that discovery come to the realization that I am a person of worth. Once I am filled with God's love, I've got something to give someone else. But many of us who have trouble loving ourselves are in fact still so self-absorbed that we're not really thinking about the other person.

It is here that Paul recommends gratitude. Be thankful, he says. I love that. Gratitude is fundamental to so much we learn in the Bible. All of Scripture calls us to live in a posture of thankfulness, first to God and then to other people. That's what we do when we gather for worship. We pause and say, "Thank you, God, for all the blessings in my life." We remember that life is a gift. And when it comes to marriage, we remember that our spouse is a gift from God.

Gratitude is key to a happy marriage. When you view something with a grateful heart, you can't take it for granted anymore. When you're constantly thanking God for your mate, you don't treat him or her poorly but instead begin to treasure what you share together.

LaVon and I pray together nearly every night, then she goes to bed, and I stay up for another hour or two. When I finally tiptoe into the bedroom, it's pitch dark and LaVon is asleep.

I get down on my knees once more and say, "God, thank you for today. Thank you for my kids and for the church." I walk through the day in my mind, and before I say amen I stop and listen to my wife's breathing. Then I say, "God, thank you for giving me the gift of LaVon. Help me to love her well. Help me to bless her. Help me to be faithful to her."

The two most important words you can say in your marriage are "Thank you."

It's funny: When I say that prayer on my knees in the middle of the night, it doesn't matter if we had an argument earlier in the evening or if we were frustrated with each other that day. Somehow the act of thanking God for my wife makes me appreciate her again. Giving thanks makes our hearts glad and grateful.

But we can't just say it to God. We have to say it to each other as well, because our surveys showed that one of the most frustrating things for both men and women is to feel unappreciated. The two most important words you can say in your marriage are "Thank you." Make it a practice to look in your spouse's eyes every day and say, "I really appreciate you. Thank you for what you've done for me." It will lighten your spouse's heart, and it will lighten yours as well.

In this book we have dealt with the nature of love and marriage and have explored what long-term relationships look like. We have talked about what helps them and what gets in the way. In all that we have discussed, though, nothing is more important than this: In order to love selflessly, to be able to clothe yourself in those virtues Paul describes, to be the husband or wife you need to be, you must have God's help.

Having a relationship with God before you have a relationship with your mate gives you the capacity to love her or him well. There is something about holding hands and praying together that binds you as a couple. There is something about sitting next to each other in church that connects you in a way nothing else can. In my own life I've found that I'm a better husband because I love God. I'm a better father because I follow Jesus Christ. I'm more faithful to LaVon because of my faith in God.

We got married as teenagers. We would not be married today if we didn't share a common faith, pray together, and serve God together. Without those things, there were times when I would have gone in another direction. I would have been unfaithful to her if my primary allegiance had not been to Jesus Christ, who called me to love my wife even when I didn't feel like it.

The people in our survey said the same thing. Of those who rarely or never attended worship together, 32 percent said they were happily married; of those who attended worship together every weekend, 50 percent were happily married. Of those who seldom or never prayed together, 35 percent said they were happily married; of those who prayed together daily, 63 percent said they were happily married.

A University of Virginia survey asked the same questions. Couples who said that God was at the center of their relationship scored 26 percent higher in marital happiness than those who didn't.[26] Whether you explain it in psychological or spiritual terms, it is real. There is a connection between God and marital happiness.

In the course of a lifetime, married couples tend to grow in different directions. LaVon and I are not the same people we were at seventeen and eighteen. We don't think the same way. Our politics, our theology — all of it's different. The one thing that's the same as when we were teenagers is that the deepest desire both LaVon and I have, the most fundamental principle of our lives, is to follow Jesus Christ. Over the years, we've found that something interesting has happened. The closer we get to Jesus Christ, the closer we are to one another. I believe this is what the apostle Paul was teaching us. It's also what one couple told us who had been married for more than sixty years:

> We would never have survived all these years, I know,
> if it hadn't been for faith. You have to continue to love
> one another. That's so important. And show each other
> how much you love them. But you also know that there's
> somebody there that's bigger than you, that no matter what
> you go through, you feel like he's put you together and he's
> going to be there for you.

The most important date you have each week is when you go to church together. I invite you to make it a priority. Hold hands during worship. Sing and pray, then afterward talk about what you heard. Couples who grow closer to Christ can't help but grow closer to each other.

A couple named Ray and Betty were members of our church for many years. It was obvious even after more than sixty years of marriage that they were very much in love. Betty passed away a couple of years ago. I asked Ray, who still is a regular in worship, for his thoughts on marriage, and this what he told me:

I believe that great marriages are divided into three phases. First is the honeymoon phase, when couples are madly in love but most of the attraction is physical. Next is the family phase, when both husband and wife are so busy with children and career that they don't have time for each other like they previously had. They grow apart somewhat. The final phase is the best of all. The family is raised and the children are developing their own lives. Husband and wife rediscover each other and are able to enjoy what they've accomplished with their marriage.

Ray went on to say, "A short time before I lost Betty, she looked at me and said, 'Ray, this was the best time of all.' At the end, we felt like we were that young couple all over again, madly in love with each other."

Ray captured the hope and vision I have for marriage, my own and yours. It is what Robert Browning pointed to in his well-known poem, "Rabbi Ben Ezra," when he wrote:

> Grow old along with me!
> The best is yet to be,

The last of life, for which the first was made:
Our times are in his hand
Who saith, "A whole I planned,
Youth shows but half; trust God: see all, nor be afraid!"[27]

My hope and prayer for you as married couples is that you will grow old along with one another. The best is yet to be.

Reflect and Engage

Love Letters

Love is a funny thing. We know that real love is put into action whether or not we feel sentimental about our partner at the moment, but those sentimental feelings can sometimes flood over us when we least expect it. It could happen when seeing your spouse interact with your children, hearing a song you listened to when you first fell in love, or watching a movie with a touching story of marital perseverance.

Those sights and experiences spark a chemical response in our brain. This may sound like a cold and technical way to talk about love, but the good news is that because of this biological response, we can sometimes trick ourselves into feeling things that we might not be feeling at the moment. Like buying flowers and a card for your spouse when you feel anything but loving, the very act of doing something romantic can make us feel more affectionate.

Words are powerful, however, so start by writing a thank-you letter to your spouse, describing things you can honestly affirm about him or her. Even if it takes a while to think of things, sit with this exercise and ponder your partner's character, talents, physical attributes, personality quirks, and daily actions. Your sentences don't have to be eloquent or grammatically correct, and your penmanship doesn't have to be neat. Just focus on blessing your spouse with your words and knowing that you mean, in your heart, what you write.

When you finish, read your letters aloud to one another, or allow the other to read silently. Thank each other for the words you have expressed. Discuss the experience afterwards with the following questions.

- What did you feel when you began this task? Did your feelings change as you were writing?
- What things did you most appreciate about what your partner wrote? Did he or she affirm things you thought had gone unnoticed? How did you feel about your partner when you read his or her words?
- How important are romantic feelings to you in your relationship and your ability to love and serve one another? How can you enhance those feelings for one another to help carry you through the more difficult periods of your marriage?

Pray Together

Dear God, thank you for our marriage and for all the wonderful gifts and qualities of my partner. Help us to show love regardless of feelings and, in the showing of love, to rediscover our feelings for one another. Grant us gracious perseverance through all the seasons of marriage, and teach us every day to love more like you. Amen.

On Your Own

Identify something that arouses sentimental, romantic feelings toward your spouse. Is it a song or movie? A memory from when you were dating? A fun trip you took together? Remember that thing so you can think about it when you feel that the "spark" is missing. Use the feelings it evokes to help you grow closer to your spouse again.

If You're Single

Write a letter to your future spouse, expressing your love, joy, and commitment as you imagine those feelings at some point in the future. Include a few lines about the way you envision working through trials in life together. While you're in letter-writing mode, pen another letter or two to a parent, friend, or significant other to express your appreciation and care.

ACKNOWLEDGMENTS

I am grateful to my wife LaVon, who allowed me to share our life experiences and stories in the hope that by sharing them, others might be encouraged or helped. I am also profoundly grateful to the 5,184 people at The Church of the Resurrection and across the country who took our survey that provided such important data for this book. Throughout the book there are stories of people whose lives have profoundly shaped my understanding of love and marriage. I am grateful for each of these.

Thanks to Rob Simbeck, who took my sermon manuscripts and from them crafted the first draft of this book; and to Matt Kelley and Jessica Kelley, who created the activities for couples at the end of each chapter. A special word of thanks to the terrific team at Abingdon Press who made this a better book by their editorial process, especially Ron Kidd, my editor; and Susan Salley, whose vision and encouragement are gifts to every author who works with her.

APPENDIX A

LOVE, SEX, AND MARRIAGE SURVEY (EXCERPTS)

Survey Background

The original research findings reported in *Love to Stay: Sex, Grace, and Commitment* are from an online survey conducted from December 2011 through February 2012. Married, single, and widowed adults were invited to participate through the websites and newsletters of The United Methodist Church of the Resurrection in Leawood, Kansas, and of author Adam Hamilton.

Survey Demographics

The survey respondents came from a variety of locations. The majority attend the Leawood campus of The United Methodist Church of the Resurrection or other campuses connected to the congregation in the Kansas City area. Twenty-six percent (26%) of the survey respondents attend other congregations around the country and globe or participate in worship online.

Survey respondents:

- 65% Attend The Church of the Resurrection, Leawood
- 9% Attend other campuses of The Church of the Resurrection around Kansas City
- 6% Participate in worship online from a variety of locations
- 20% Attend other congregations around country and globe

The survey consists of 5,184 respondents, including:

3,856	married adults
927	single adults
274	partnered or cohabitating adults
127	widows and widowers
5,184	

More women (63%) participated than men (37%), and the majority of respondents were between thirty and fifty-nine years of age.

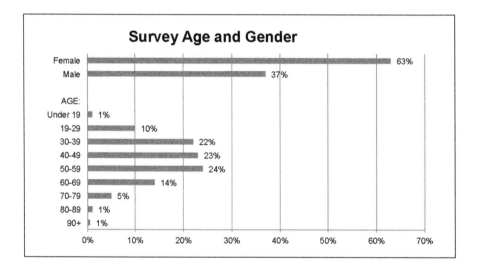

Key Questions for Singles

The majority of the nearly 1,000 singles answering the online survey plan to get married. The traits these men and women look for most in a potential spouse are trustworthiness, honesty, and a strong faith. Their biggest turnoffs, with respondents selecting up to three choices from a list, included judgmental behavior, arrogance, and bad habits (smoking or drinking too much, bad grooming, rudeness to others).

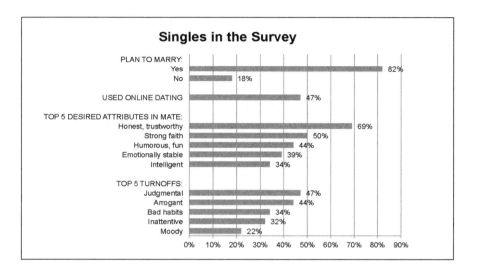

Men and women differed somewhat in their ranking of desired attributes and turnoffs. While both sexes are interested in honesty, faith and a good sense of humor, men ranked physical appearance in their top five responses while women included emotional stability and good communication skills.

Desired Attributes in a Mate	Men	Women
	Honest, Trustworthy	Honest, Trustworthy
	Physically Attractive	Strong Faith
	Strong Faith	Humorous, Fun
	Humorous, Fun	Emotionally Stable
	Intelligent	Good Communicator

Top Five Turnoffs	Men	Women
	Close-minded/Judgmental	Arrogant/Bragging
	Moody	Close-minded/Judgmental
	Arrogant/Bragging	Bad Habits
	Bad Habits	Not Listening/Inattentive
	Not Fun	Sexually Aggressive

Key Questions for Divorced People
Of the total respondents to the survey, whether married, single or
widowed today, thirty-one percent had experienced divorce. The
majority divorced in the first five years of marriage. When describing in
their own words the leading cause of their own divorce, infidelity was
the top response followed by addictions and abuse.

Have you ever been divorced? (n=4,314)

Yes	31%

Years married to the first spouse

2 years or less	19%
2 to 5 years	21%
6 to 10 years	22%
11 to 20 years	30%
21 to 30 years	13%
31 to 40 years	3%
41 to 50 years	1%

Leading cause of the divorce

Infidelity	16%
Alcohol or substance abuse	9%
Physical/emotional abuse	7%
Too young, immature	6%
Money, finances	5%
Communication, listening	4%
Mental illness	3%

Key Questions for Married People

A total of 3,856 married individuals responded to the survey, though as you can see in the graphs below, not every individual answered all the questions. Nearly half of the respondents have been married between 11 and 30 years. Thirty-six percent (36%) of married individuals had lived with their spouses before they married.

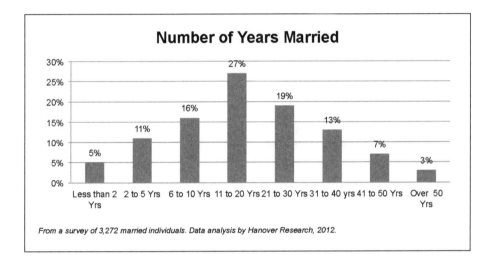

From a survey of 3,272 married individuals. Data analysis by Hanover Research, 2012.

The couples in the sample are clearly more involved in church and church-related activities than a secular group might be:

Frequency of Worship Attendance

	Self	Spouse
Weekly, unless sick or away	54%	49%
Regularly	28%	27%
Monthly	9%	9%
Rarely	8%	12%
Never	1%	3%

Frequency of Prayer Together with Spouse

More than 1 time/day	2%
Daily	17%
At least weekly	16%
Seldom	37%
Never	27%

Tithe (Give 10% of Income)	39%

Attend Small Group Study Together	28%

Have Taken a Mission Trip Together	11%

Most of the survey respondents are in happy relationships with more than 75% describing their marriages as happy or mostly happy. Only 6% report that their relationships are getting worse with time. When comparing the responses from married men and women, men are more likely to report being very happy or that their marriages are improving.

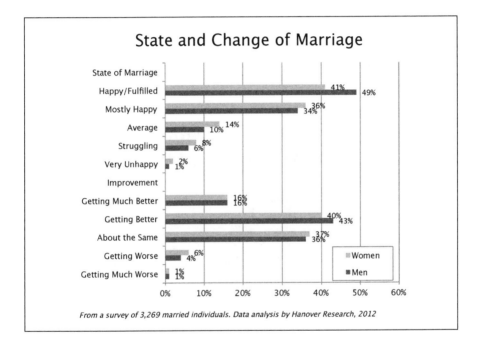

From a survey of 3,269 married individuals. Data analysis by Hanover Research, 2012

Date night. Intentional time together varies also with only one in five people reporting a weekly "date."

Frequency of Dates with My Spouse (n=3,237)

Weekly	20%
Twice a month	15%
Monthly	22%
About six times a year	20%
Rarely	21%
Never	2%

Sexual Relationships

The range of satisfaction with the physical dimension of relationships varies among married respondents though more people report being satisfied than unsatisfied. Men are slightly more likely to report dissatisfaction than women. The frequency of sexual intimacy also varies greatly with about one fourth reporting physical intimacy at least weekly.

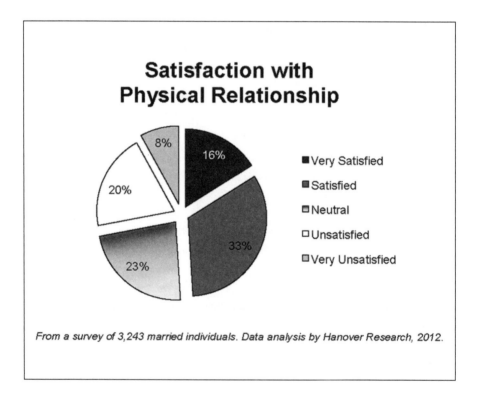

From a survey of 3,243 married individuals. Data analysis by Hanover Research, 2012.

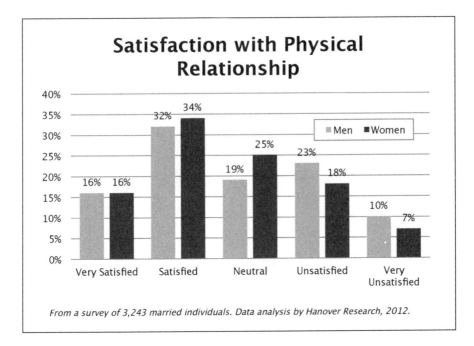

From a survey of 3,243 married individuals. Data analysis by Hanover Research, 2012.

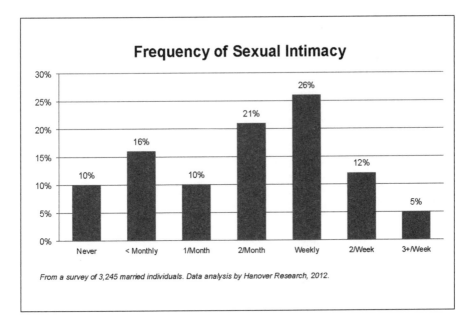

From a survey of 3,245 married individuals. Data analysis by Hanover Research, 2012.

Conflict in Marriage

Half of the married respondents report conflict with their spouses "rarely" or "never," and the majority describes the conflict that does occur as minor. The method of dealing with conflict—including silence, talking, or avoidance—varies widely. Only 2% report conflicts as becoming physical.

Frequency of Conflict with a Spouse (n=3,247)

Several Times/Day	1%
Daily	4%
Several Times/Week	14%
Weekly	29%
Rarely	50%
Never	1%

Severity of Most Conflicts (n=3,224)

Minor	83%
Somewhat Serious	15%
Very Serious	2%

Spouse's Primary Way of Responding (n=3,237)

Talking It Through	31%
Avoidance	26%
Angry Outburst	25%
Silent treatment	14%
Other	8%

Does Conflict Become Physical?

Yes	2%

Married respondents considered a list of possible causes of conflict
in marriage. When respondents were asked to select up to three
regular sources of conflict and one single greatest source of conflict,
communication and a failure to listen topped the list in each category.

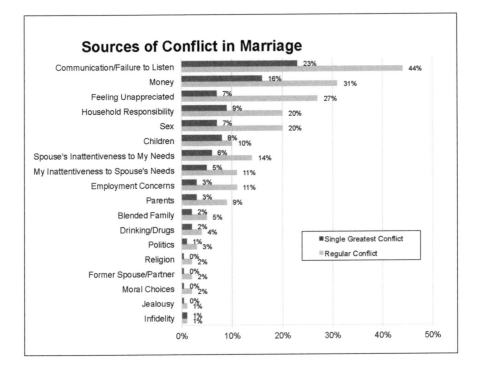

Improving the Relationship

When asked the one thing that a mate does to make his or her partner feel closer, the activities respondents mentioned most often were "share thoughts and feelings" and "demonstrate affection." The things that spouses would most like their mates to do more frequently include "sexual intimacy" (mentioned by one in four respondents) and "demonstrate affection."

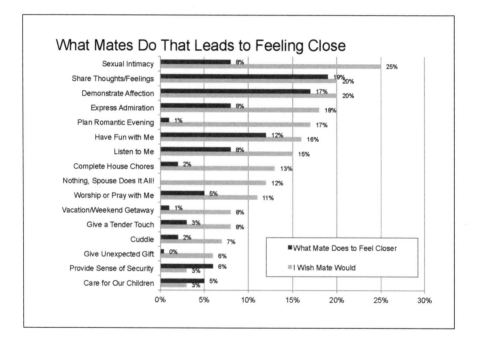

Comparing the responses from men and women on the one thing that their mate does that makes them feel closer to each other, there are some key differences. The top two responses from men are "demonstrating affection" and "sexual intimacy." For women, the top two are "sharing thoughts and feelings" and "demonstrating affection."

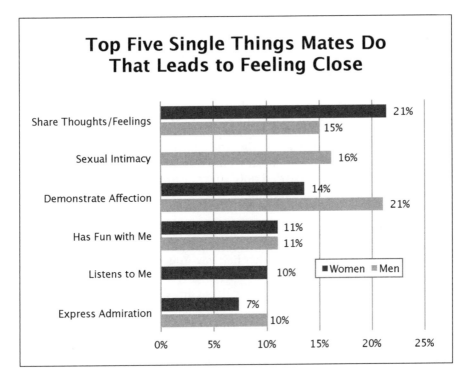

Appendix B

Advice of Couples Married 50+ Years

Nearly 100 married individuals in the survey group had been married to their spouses for fifty years or more. At the end of the survey, these couples shared advice by answering the question: "As someone who has been married 50+ years, what would you say to newlyweds and to people who've been married only a few years about what it takes to make a marriage last for a lifetime?"

Here are some of their candid responses for readers of *Love to Stay*.

- You both have to meet each other halfway. You both have to give in once in a while.
- To care for each other and always talk out any differences and feelings each day.
- Always be true to each other, and work through problems no matter what!!! He used to have a difficult time talking things out but the years have made him much, much better.
- Things are never fifty/fifty. There has to be a lot of give and take. Say you love each other every day. Make sure you both know your financial situation so you both can know when to spend and when not to spend. Keep Christ as the head of the house. Laugh a lot with each other. Know when each of you is teasing so you won't become offended. Learn to take teasing and laugh at yourself. AND love, love, love.
- Show & express your love OFTEN. Have lots of sex and act like lovers. Show & express your pride & admiration in/for your spouse. Talk lots and share your real feelings & needs in non-accusatory ways. Plan and talk often about prudent management of your finances. Love & care for your children. Worship and pray together every week.
- Respect each other and care for each other.
- Put Christ first in your life and marriage, then all will follow.
- Worship together, pray at meals and other times, converse constantly, have fun, be angry at the situation and don't take it out on the spouse but when you do make sure they know you are venting at the situation. Talk to a counselor some times. Talk to each other and not some other person about your challenges.
- Be honest have fun.

- Respect each other and accept them for who they are. Stay out of debt and share with each other as in a partnership.
- Both partners must participate at any time, any place, any hour of the day, ANY time there is a need. You must know that being there for each other is the most important part of a marriage. Marriage is a partnership—not to be taken lightly. You must eat, breath, and live, worship in the same space.
- Remember the qualities that drew you together in the beginning of your relationship. Put Christ at the center of your home and your relationship. Not every day is perfect, have a sense of humor, spend more time counting the good than the bad! Show respect to one another.
- Don't get caught up in trivial matters. Give attention to one another. Time is always on your side.
- Always put the other first.
- Hang in there! No marriage is ideal and it just takes a lot of patience, commitment, and strong sense of the family unit to keep it together. Pretty sure we both feel after all these years our children and grandchildren would just be devastated if we separated. We hope to make this commitment a good role model to extended family. Crossed fingers!!!! So far it's worked.
- Kiss her every night before going to bed.
- Both parties must work at making it work; if a problem appears, it must be promptly addressed, to the satisfaction of both.
- Forgive and forget. Don't hold grudges. Be friends.
- I am glad I can look back and say . . . we NEVER had disagreements about our faith or money. Discuss both subjects in full and agree on them before you say…I DO! Don't look for stupid stuff to fight about. It is so much easier to live with someone you can agree with on some ways to spend your free time, hobbies, travel, kinds of friends and what you like to do for fun. A VALUE SYSTEM in common is VERY important!
- Go to church together. Be faithful. Forget small disagreements and work together
- Listen - Listen - Listen to all of your spouse's concerns. Talk through any problems.
- Take time to "talk," and try to have fun. Life is short, so try to not be so serious all the time, It really isn't hard if you're kind to one another and show each other how you feel, not only with sex, but it's the little things like a wink, or a pat.

NOTES

1. National Marriage Project, "2011 The State of Our Unions: Marriage in America," accessed May 22, 2013, http://www.stateofourunions.org/2011/SOOU2011.pdf, 67.
2. D'Vera Cohn, Jeffrey Passel, Wendy Wang, and Gretchen Livingston, "Barely Half of U.S. Adults Are Married — A Record Low," accessed May 22, 2013, http://www.pewsocialtrends.org/2011/12/14/barely-half-of-u-s-adults-aremarried-a-record-low.
3. "Divorce Rate," accessed May 24, 2013, http://www.divorce.com/article/divorce-rate.
4. The Pew Research Center, "The Decline of Marriage And Rise of New Families," 2010.
5. Gary Chapman, *Love Languages* (Chicago: Northfield, 1992).
6. Gary Chapman, "Discover Your Love Language," accessed May 24, 2013, http://www.5lovelanguages.com.
7. Barbara De Angelis uses this metaphor throughout her book *What Women Want Men to Know* (New York: Hyperion, 2001). Willard F. Harley, Jr. discusses it extensively in his book *His Needs, Her Needs: Building an Affair-Proof Marriage* (Grand Rapids, MI: Revell, 2011).
8. Rollo May, *Love and Will* (New York: W.W. Norton, 1969), 65.
9. Laura Roberts, "Couples Who Don't Have Sex Before Marriage Are Happier, Study Claims," *The Telegraph*, accessed May 24, 2013, http://www.telegraph.co.uk/health/healthnews/8226959/Couples-who-dont-have-sex-before-marriage-are-happier-study-claims.html.
10. David Snarch, *Intimacy and Desire* (New York: Beaufort, 2009).
11. Arkansas Coalition Against Domestic Violence "National Domestic Violence Statistics," accessed May 27, 2013, http://www.domesticpeace.com/ed_nationalstats.html.
12. John Gottman and Nan Silver, *The Seven Principles for Making Marriage Work* (New York: Three Rivers, 1999), 2.
13. Shelley Lubben,"The Truth Behind the Fantasy of Porn," accessed May 27, 2013, http://www.cbn.com/700club/features/thetruth_lubben.aspx.
14. T.C. Ryan, *Ashamed No More: A Pastor's Journey Through Sex Addiction* (Downers Grove, Ill.: Intervarsity, 2012).
15. Infidelity Help Group,"Infidelity Statistics," accessed May 27, 2013, http://www.infidelityhelpgroup.com/infidelity-help-statistics/5/.
16. Rita Watson, "Low Infidelity, Shock Statistics, and the Forgiveness Factor," accessed May 27, 2013, http://www.psychologytoday.com/blog/love-and-gratitude/201109/low-infidelity-shock-statistics-and-the-forgiveness-factor.
17. Pat Fagan and Althea Nagai, "Adultery by Religious Attendance," Mapping America: Marriage, Religion and the Common Good 73, accessed May 27, 2013, http://marri.us/get.cfm?i=MA09J01.

18. Walter Wangerin, Jr., *As For Me And My House: Crafting Your Marriage To Last* (Nashville: Thomas Nelson, 1990), 196.
19. JuJu Chang, "Facebook Infidelity: Cheating Spouses Go Online," accessed May 27, 2013, http://abcnews.go.com/Technology/facebook-infidelity-cheatingspouses-online/story?id=12272421.
20. Nancy Gibbs and Richard N. Ostling, "God's Billy Pulpit," *Time*, November 15, 1993, accessed May 30, 2013, http://www.angelfire.com/zine/baptistsurfer/TimeGraham.html.
21. Sam Margulies, "The Annual Marital Performance Review," accessed May 27, 2013, http://www.psychologytoday.com/blog/divorce-grownups/201002/the-annual-marital-performance-review
22. Gottman and Silver, 149.
23. Mark Morris, "Three-year term in fatal gunplay," *The Kansas City Star*, February 4, 2012, A-1.
24. Gottman and Silver, 27.
25. Composed by Alan Bergman, Marilyn Bergman, and Neil Diamond, "You Don't Bring Me Flowers," Neil Diamond and Barbra Streisand, *Barbra Streisand's Greatest Hits Volume 2*, Columbia, 1978.
26. National Marriage Project, "2011 The State of Our Unions: Marriage in America," accessed May 27, 2013, http://www.stateofourunions.org/2011/SOOU2011.pdf, 31.
27. Robert Browning, *Rabbi Ben Ezra: A Dramatic Monologue* (BiblioBazaar, 2009).

ENOUGH

With more than 120,000 copies sold since its initial 2009 release, *Enough* has changed countless lives by offering hope, spiritual direction, and assurance that anyone can, with God's help, find his or her way to a place of financial peace and contentment.

In this new and expanded hardcover edition, Adam Hamilton shows there is a way back to a firm spiritual and financial foundation. In these pages, readers can find the keys to experiencing contentment, overcoming fear, and discovering joy through simplicity and generosity.

This book will change your life by changing your relationship with money.

ISBN 978-1-4267-4207-1

AVAILABLE WHEREVER FINE BOOKS ARE SOLD.
FOR MORE INFORMATION ABOUT ADAM HAMILTON, VISIT WWW.ADAMHAMILTON.ORG

FORGIVENESS

Adam Hamilton equates our
need to forgive and be forgiven
with carrying a backpack filled with
rocks. Over time the tiny pebbles
and giant boulders weigh us down
and break more than our spirit. In
*Forgiveness: Finding Peace Through Letting
Go,* Hamilton shows readers how to
receive the freedom that comes with
forgiving—even if the person needing
forgiveness is ourselves.

Read *Forgiveness* on your own or, for
a more in-depth study, enjoy it with a
small group.

ISBN 978-1-4267-4044-2

AVAILABLE WHEREVER FINE BOOKS ARE SOLD.
FOR MORE INFORMATION ABOUT ADAM HAMILTON, VISIT WWW.ADAMHAMILTON.ORG

WHY?
MAKING SENSE OF GOD'S WILL

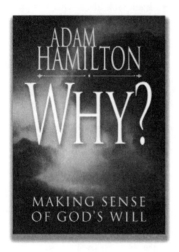

When the ground shakes, and a poor nation's economy is destroyed; when the waters rise, washing away a community's hopes and dreams; when a child suffers neglect and abuse; when violence tears apart nations: Where is God?

In *Why? Making Sense of God's Will*, bestselling author Adam Hamilton brings fresh insight to the age-old question of how to understand the will of God. Rejecting simplistic answers and unexamined assumptions, Hamilton addresses how we can comprehend God's plan for the world and ourselves.

"I recommend this book to anyone who longs to leave behind simplistic answers and discover a God who invites them into a collaborative process of bringing redemption, love, and hope to a world in desperate need." —**Lynne Hybels**, author of *Nice Girls Don't Change the World*

ISBN 978-1-4267-1478-8

੨।Abingdon Press™

AVAILABLE WHEREVER FINE BOOKS ARE SOLD.
FOR MORE INFORMATION ABOUT ADAM HAMILTON, VISIT WWW.ADAMHAMILTON.ORG